the treasury of
Kittens

the treasury o

Kittens

Marjorie Hudson

Octopus Books

First published in Great Britain in 1973 by
Octopus Books Ltd
59 Grosvenor Street, London, W.1.

© Octopus Books Limited

ISBN 0 7064 0084 4

Produced by Mandarin Publishers Limited
77a Marble Road, North Point, Hong Kong.

Printed in Hong Kong

Contents

Choosing a kitten 6

Pedigree kittens 28

First days with your kitten 46

Life with your kitten 66

Breeding and rearing the kittens 92

Boarding catteries 124

Choosing a kitten

So you want a cat, or rather a kitten, who in course of time will become that most elusive and dignified of all animals. What kind of kitten do you want and why? It is important to stop and think about this for a little while before you acquire a kitten. It may seem very obvious to say that your kitten will grow into a cat but it cannot be said too often. A cat will live for anything up to 10–23 years and for that time you will always be responsible for its happiness and well-being, so that arrangements must be made when you go away even for a short time. Then, do you want an 'ordinary' cat or would you like a valuable pedigree and if you have a long-hair will you have time to groom it? If you have a female, do you want to breed from her or would it be better to have her spayed? These considerations must be taken into account before it is too late and you are forced to give away your cat or worse, have it put down.

You may, of course, acquire your kitten without any choice – many poor little 'scraps' are abandoned every year and many a beautiful cat started life as an unwanted waif left in a ditch before being rescued by one of the many societies or dedicated people who take in these creatures and find them homes or put them painlessly to sleep. All cat lovers will thank those who take a stray into their home and thereby rescue even one of these results of man's inhumanity. Perhaps you have been offered a non-pedigree kitten, one of a litter, and you are able to choose the colour you prefer or perhaps one of the kittens will 'choose' you. What-

ever determines your choice, children often fall for one particular kitten and it is very hard to resist that apparent 'love at first sight'.

As Christmas draws near, many kittens go to new homes – often as presents to children, and it is wonderful for children to grow up with young animals. The children learn responsibility, toleration and love for small creatures through daily contact. A great many of these kittens remain loved pets, giving in return warm affection and the happiness desired. But here I must include a word of warning. Kittens grow and become cats and in many cases children and even adults lose interest as the kitten

develops from a little ball of fur into a larger, less playful animal. Or else they find that the kitten has habits of which they disapprove, like climbing curtains or scratching furniture. Even the regular feeding or changing of litter pans can become just one more chore for a busy mother. So if you are a prospective cat owner you must be prepared for all these things or you may be tempted to commit the cruel crime of allowing an innocent, happy kitten to become one of the thousands of homeless, unwanted, hungry cats of next year. Will you feel that the necessary precautions to prevent litters of unwanted kittens are too much bother or too expensive? Only you

A litter of Silver Tabby kittens. At this age they all look alike, but will already be different in character.

can decide not to add to the number of unwanted animals.

Now if you decided to go on and have a kitten (and no doubt you will have if you are truly a cat lover) the choice is yours and there is a vast field open to you, as well as a great many things you will want to know. I shall be writing in another chapter about pedigree kittens; meanwhile, there are some basic rules which should be followed by all would-be owners.

Kittens should be at least eight weeks old before leaving their mother. Although many strays are abandoned earlier than this and survive, it is better for the kitten to be fully weaned from his mother before having to cope with the stress of leaving her and his brothers and sisters, as well as the major changes of a new environment and possibly a complete change of food. If you have rescued a kitten, a visit to your local vet is a good idea. He will advise you of its age, sex and health, for it may need extra care after the probable hardship of its early life.

Your next move is to decide whether you want a male or female. If you are going to have a non-pedigree kitten, you will probably be wanting him or her as a pet. If you have a female you may think that later on it would be fun to have perhaps one litter of kittens; but if you think this please also think of the kittens' future, of the many Toms that will haunt your home and of whether you have the time to devote to very young animals. I am assuming that you will be sensible, and with your own interests and probably those of your cat at heart, you will decide to have her spayed – what the Americans call 'altered' – or if you have a male, neutered.

May I add here the strongest plea that this operation should be carried out. Unwanted litters are a tragedy as they are either drowned or become strays. All those who keep unneutered males are contributing to this tragedy as your Tom will undoubtedly do his best to contribute largely to the population of strays, and it is quite impossible to find homes for the majority of these kittens.

Quite apart from this, there are other most unpleasant habits associated with full males. They wander away, seeking females in season and sometimes, in desperation, will even try mating females who are not. I once had a young female, seven weeks pregnant, who was forcibly mated by a farm cat and so badly mauled in resisting that two days later she had a miscarriage. As usually happens, her six premature kittens died one by one. I may add that she never had another litter, although this may have had no connection with her accident.

Unneutered males can ruin a home

Above, a frightened long-haired cat preparing to defend himself. Right, a ginger and white kitten and below, a Long-haired Cream kitten.
Next page, Tabby and White Longhairs.

by 'spraying' everywhere. This spray is most pungent and unpleasant. The strong smell is entirely resistant to washing or disinfectants. No blame can be attached to the cat, he is just following his normal sexual pattern. Spray scent marks out his territory and will warn any other wandering male to keep out! Such a male will roam for miles and become a fighter, sueing for the favour of females, courting the lady of his choice during the night and then perhaps returning home after a long absence. During this time he will have encountered other males with the same objective and will inevitably become battle torn and 'tatty'.

I have had many discussions and arguments with men on the cruelty of neutering males (not females mark you). There have been many and varied reasons put forward why this

Above, two beautiful kittens from a mixed litter.

Above left, a ginger kitten, and below, a mixed litter with their giant companion, a Great Dane.

should not be done including the old chestnut 'He won't hunt any more'. This is absolute nonsense. There is no cruelty involved at all and anyone arguing against neutering must to my mind then answer for the treatment that is so often meted out to unwanted kittens – I have known them dumped down a lavatory pan when born, or thrown into a ditch, or drowned. The cat's temperament is changed only in so far as he is more gentle, clean and does not wander. He will hunt as well as ever – after all, it isn't his hunting instinct which is affected. I find that farmers are the worst culprits against neutering.

If you have a female kitten the case is as strong because of the problems of unwanted kittens. She will have a great many litters – more than will be good for her – unless you have her spayed. Her operation is rather more serious, but nowadays is almost as safe as neutering. Nor will it affect her character and once your female has fully recovered from her operation and is back to her normal playful habits, there will be no noticeable change in her temperament. If however, you decide at some time to have an older cat spayed, and this can be done up until the cat is five or six years old, then you will notice slight changes. She may, unless you limit her food to half an ounce per pound body weight, grow fatter and more placid, but certainly not less playful. One of the delights of a spayed female is the vast improvement in her coat. For some reason, and I suspect it is hormonal, her fur becomes glossy and fine – in fact, without the stress of

continual calling and perhaps kittening, she becomes a creature of tremendous life and health.

Finally you need not worry that non-pedigree kittens, as a species, will become extinct. No fear of that whilst we have Farmer Giles with his barns – a veritable paradise for indiscriminate breeding – and the thousands of abandoned animals of which I spoke earlier.

Talking of persistent Tom cats, as they are commonly called, I once had a rather sweet stray around my cattery, who would visit us frequently before any of the females came into season and whose daily visits would cease only when the call of the female in question finished. One day two Siamese females, a Chocolate Point and a Tortie Point came into season simultaneously. I therefore put them both into a house in the cattery where they would sit on the shelf in their little garden, serenading anyone who would listen – as if one could get away

13

Above, an adopted stray Burmese cat and her attractive mixed litter. Two of the kittens have the 'M' markings of true Tabbies on their foreheads, and one has Siamese markings (below). The Burmese mother is thin and in bad condition as any stray will be, but she looks after her kittens as well as the most coddled, home-loving cats, and is here carrying the Siamese kitten of the litter back to the nest. Right and over the page, the family . . .

from that sound. I saw the old Tom patiently crouched in the grass, with his nose pressed to the wire run and his eyes abrim with love. He did not mind which one he mated, and he was perfectly willing to set up a 'ménage à trois'.

He sat there all day, and I confidently believed that when night came he would return to whichever barn he happened to call home at that time, but I was wrong. In the morning he was still there, same place, same position, same conversation. The 'girls' greeted him ecstatically and that night I again thought he would go. However, there he was, back again on the third day, and I could not stand it any longer for my

poor old Tom was getting thinner by the hour. I was no doubt very stupid, for I then fed him and continued to do so during the whole of his long vigil, a matter of six days and nights. On the eighth day, I released the 'girls' and all was back to normal – Tom disappeared and the females came into the house.

Four weeks later, I noticed the Tortie Point looking remarkably well. She had put on weight which pleased me because she was normally such a skinny cat. Six weeks passed and I realized the Tom's patience had been rewarded, but when or how, I was, and still am, at a complete loss to understand. Sure enough, on the 66th day after their release from the cat-

. . . out exploring the garden. The Burmese parentage of these strays can be seen in their oriental eyes and pointed faces.

tery, Cleo went into labour, presenting me with nine wonderfully assorted kittens, each and every one different and all perfectly beautiful.

Oh Tom – you wily old cat – and to think I even fed you! But it is plain that persistence pays.

When your kitten reaches the age of about five to six months, contact your vet and ask him if he will perform the necessary operation. Do not do so before this age as the kitten is

Two Long-haired Tabby kittens about six months old.

not fully developed and if a male is neutered too early it can cause trouble with his bladder etc, when he is older. Your vet will ask you to bring the kitten to his surgery. He will probably warn you, but if he does not, remember not to give the kitten any food at all on the morning he goes for his operation, not even a drink of milk. Put him into the cat basket which I hope you remembered to buy, on a warm blanket and, without fuss or agitation, quietly take him to the surgery and hand him over.

He will be well treated and feel no pain, for the law now insists that all cats and kittens must be given an anaesthetic before this operation is performed. You will probably be allowed to bring him home later that evening. He may appear a little un-steady on his legs, so tuck him up warmly in his bed and let him sleep. He will soon be loudly demanding food, telling you in no uncertain terms that he is starving.

If it is a female going to be spayed, the procedure is much the same – no food. As her operation is a little more complicated, your vet may well decide to keep her in his surgery over-night. If he does, not to worry, she will be kept warm and quiet and will quickly recover from the anaesthetic

whilst there. When you bring her home you will find she has a small shaven patch on her left side. There will be a slight cut of about one to one and a half inches, sewn with two or three stitches. She will not appear ill, only slightly reluctant for 24 hours to play in her usual fashion. She may or may not eat, but will probably welcome a drink of, say Brand's Essence, or milk if she is accustomed to it.

Within 48 hours, your kitten will probably be full of beans again, none

the worse for her 'surgical'. In a week's time, the vet will want to see her to remove the stitches, so try to get her there on the appointed day just in case she decides to take them out herself. If by chance she has found them irritating and has endeavoured to remove them herself, don't panic, take her into the surgery again and let your vet see for himself.

I want to tell you about an incident which made a lasting impression upon me and which might help you

to understand my pleas for the spaying or neutering of pets: some years ago my husband came in from the garden and said that he had seen a stray kitten behind the compost heap, but that it was so shy that he couldn't get near it. For several days he reported catching quick glimpses of the little thing, which was undoubtedly feeding from the rubbish on the compost heap. Eventually, it became tame enough to remain eating whilst he watched and then I joined him and between us we tried to get a closer view of the kitten's condition.

As time went on I became extremely concerned for its welfare for I realized this 'kitten' was in fact about five months old and literally starving. I fell in love with her fragile beauty as she grew daily less nervous of me. By this time she would wait each evening for me to bring a plate of meat or milk, and although I did not attempt to touch or coerce her she displayed her gratitude with purrs of thanks, rolling over on her poor bony little back and sometimes following me down through the garden to the house. Here she would stop as though she knew – as I did – that she was 'unclean'. The humility of that little creature who would stand away, out of contact of our own well fed animals,

and yet who obviously yearned to join in was more than I could bear. I soon realized to my horror that the kitten was herself pregnant, so I managed to coax her to me and together we went to my vet. He examined her, confirmed that she was six weeks pregnant although herself only a kitten and that through starvation her bones were malformed. She had a heart murmur, mange and other complications. He said she couldn't live to give birth to her kittens and that the kindest thing was to put her to sleep.

Supposing you already have one cat and wish to bring a new kitten into your home – how should you introduce this strange intruder to the present resident? Most people constantly dealing with cats have their own way of integration, but I have

found the following method highly satisfactory. Never allow your cat free access to the kitten for the first few hours – in fact I keep a kitten entirely separated for at least two days, after which I bring in the cat, and with the kitten on my lap formally introduce them. There will be an arched back from the kitten together with some pretty rude remarks. Curiosity will determine the extent to which the cat responds before he also, disliking the tone of voice of the interloper, will probably respond by hissing, together with a flashing paw designed to teach the young cub a lesson. Be quick, don't allow the paw to land on the kitten otherwise it will take that much longer for them to get acquainted. Fuss the cat, assuring him of your affection as ever and then terminate the interview. By this time the cat will probably have taken his leave in high dudgeon anyway. Repeat the above as often as possible, never leaving them alone together at night. Eventually, you will find them mousing together under an armchair and from then on all is well, but don't expect miracles.

Some cats take a long time to accept a newcomer, but if you treat them both in just the same way as when introducing a new baby to an older child, in other words with patience, you should be rewarded in the end. Another way is to use a small wire pet pen, but it means making it or buying it. The kitten is put safely in the pen and the cat allowed to sniff him between the wires.

The very first kitten I had was after my marriage and was a funny little black fellow bought for five shillings from a pet shop. I had no knowledge of cats for my father hated them and we were never allowed to have one in the house. Nicky, as we called him, thrived on our diet and the great affection we gave him, sleeping at the foot of our bed at night and, as he grew older, imperiously informing us when he considered it bedtime.

We had bought a plot of land and were building our first house. We had

Left, a Ginger Tom kitten who seems to have his fair share of aggressiveness. Right, a Long-haired White kitten and a Long-haired Black which is still very young since his eyes are blue. All kittens have blue eyes when they are born.

Above, a Seal Colourpoint kitten has found an ideal play thing and hiding place.

Left, two non-pedigree kittens ready for some fun and games.

to visit the site every evening to watch progress, if any, and we automatically took Nicky with us. He would jump into the back of the car and, on arrival at the site, would jump out and disappear into the surrounding woods. When we were ready to depart, a call would bring him tearing back and into the car, purring and satisfied. We did not question his obedience or his love of the car and it was only much later that we realized what an extraordinary

little cat he was. In due course, we moved into our new home, with Nicky taking possession of the saucepan shelf alongside the transom of the kitchen window, through which he would go to and fro.

He was an amazing hunter and never a day passed without his bringing back a trophy – a rabbit, a rat and unfortunately on one occasion a ringed pigeon! One day, I found Nicky on his shelf obviously guarding something and when I tried to enquire

Left, non-pedigree kittens are often more appealing than pedigrees, though these Chinchilla kittens (above) look as if they will steal the show.

what he had up there, he showed his annoyance, slapping me down with a lightning paw, his eyes like yellow fire. I left him alone and almost forgot about him until some time later, whilst busy in the kitchen, I heard to my astonishment a tiny miaow, miaow! I stood on a stool, took Nicky firmly by the scruff and lifted him from his booty. There, curled up was what looked like a ball of dirty white

angora wool – and reaching up I brought down a tiny white kitten in a pitifully emaciated state, its little frame barely covered by matted fur. I suppose the little scrap wasn't more than four weeks old and where Nicky had found him I never knew, but he had obviously been abandoned.

We cleaned and cared for the kitten with Nicky's help. He adored him and, in course of time, the two were inseparable, Nicky teaching him to hunt, although I suspect Nicky did the hunting and allowed the kitten to bring home the spoil. Eventually, Twink, as he was called, grew into a

magnificent specimen, and as a result of regular grooming and good food his coat would have rivalled that of many a long-haired show cat. He ousted Nicky from his shelf by the window, and gradually usurped Nicky's seniority in the house until one day they 'had it out', with Twink coming off second best. From that time he knew his place and the saucepan shelf was once again Nicky's.

Many hundreds of cats have passed through my hands since then, but never again have I been presented with a stray kitten to look after and feed by any one of them.

Pedigree kittens

I have talked about some of the basic considerations that prospective cat owners should take into account whatever kind of kitten or kittens they finally choose; now it is time to go further into the many different pedigree kittens available. This does not mean I want to discourage you from having a non-pedigree kitten, far from it, but I do want to talk about the fascination of owning a pedigree animal and some of the possibilities open to such owners. In the following pages I will give you a list of the pedigree breeds obtainable. Some are much rarer than others, but all are different and exciting, and most of these can give you a new interest and a lot of fun. One thing I must stress. Do not believe that by buying a female pedigree kitten and eventually having kittens of your own from her that you will make money. It never works that way, especially for beginners.

I shall start with the Siamese cat, as it is this breed that I know best. Please ask yourself whether you want a pet for company at home, for showing or for breeding. This is important. I might say that a lot of people over the past years have looked upon pedigree cats, particularly Siamese, as a status symbol, not stopping to think of their responsibility towards the animal. No one, and I repeat, no one should ever lightly undertake the acquisition of a Siamese. They are loving and cajoling, yet aloof, companionable, yet solitary. Sleek, slant-eyed, mysterious creatures of great beauty, they

Previous page, a Tabby Point Siamese Queen (mated to a Seal Point male) and her mixed litter. She is of good type, but the kittens are very round faced.

Below, an Abyssinian with her two tabby-marked kittens. These markings disappear as the kittens grow older.

A handsome Cameo cat. These are very popular in America and are a new breed not yet recognized in Britain. They have sparkling coats of varying degrees of cream and red.

are completely independent, yet still utterly dependent on human love and companionship.

When you see a Siamese – look first at the head and think of a triangle. The ears should be large, wide apart and well pricked. The face should come without a break (pinch) to a blunt point with good firm chin. The eyes must be narrow and at the same time slant towards the ears; they are a deep blue with no squint. The body must be long, lithe and firm to the touch. The back legs should be slightly higher than the front. The tail must be long and whip-like with no kink, and the feet small and oval-shaped. The coat colour is pale cream in direct contrast to the points, meaning the face, ears, legs and tail. They are sleek to the point that inexperienced people will exclaim 'Isn't your cat thin!' Pick up a foreign type kitten or cat, of whichever variety mentioned above, and if he is healthy you will feel the muscles, hard and firm beneath the silky coat. A fat oriental type cat is a tragedy and there are only three reasons for this state of affairs – overfeeding, lack of exercise, or old age, which does sometimes produce surplus weight as it does with humans.

There are many different pointed Siamese from which to choose; firstly of course, the famous Seal Point

Left, two Cream Long-haired kittens playing are joined later by a Blue Long-hair.

Below, a Havana Brown cat and kitten. This breed is a cross between a Black Long-hair and a Siamese.

which is perhaps the best known of all. Later the Blue Point was produced and this should have a paler coat – glacial white, with soft, slaty blue points and no fawn on the back. Here a slightly different eye colour is correct; it should be brilliant blue and not quite as deep as that of the Seal Point.

One of the loveliest varieties is the Chocolate Point. This cat has a cream coat with no shading, brilliant blue eyes and all points a matching chocolate. It is a difficult cat to produce, but gives one enormous satisfaction when true bred. This cat should keep its pale cream unshaded coat all its life and I have a six-year-old mother

of many kittens, some of which are illustrated here (see page 110), who has a pure, unblemished coat.

Lilac Points, just recognized and granted a breed number by the Governing Council of the Cat Fancy in 1960 are ethereal creatures, with a white coat, vivid blue eyes and points of pale pinkish mauve. A true Lilac Point is a very beautiful creature and somehow their characters are softer. I find this applies to both Chocolate and Lilac Points.

One of the newest varieties is the Tabby Point, produced quite accidentally at first by the mis-mating of a Seal Point female with what must have been a Tabby. The kittens of

this variety are real 'show stoppers' for their beauty is breathtaking. They have pale bodies with cobweb marked faces, deep sapphire, black ringed eyes, fine well ringed tails with solid black tips, black stockings up the backs of the hind legs and wide ears with black 'thumb marks' at the back. They are one of the most fascinating of all Siamese.

Red Points are one of the new and

Above, a Prussian Blue kitten.

exciting colours; imagine points the colour of red gold, and brilliant blue eyes and one has a picture of a most strikingly beautiful cat. The kittens show very little colour in their points until they are a few months old, but one should aim at a deep red gold if buying an older kitten. The Red Points I have are all delightful char- acters – gentle, loving, unafraid and very companionable. I would like now to mention one of the quaintest and sweetest of all the Siamese colours – the Tortie Point. Often laughed at, sometimes disliked, these are the most useful of all the Siamese to the serious breeder as they have evenly patched points, are usually of beautiful type, and mated to a basic colour can produce all the various points.

Then there are the Burmese – Brown, Blue and Cream; the Abyssinians (known affectionately as Abys) – Nor- mal and Red; the Rex (curly coated), Devon and Cornish, in many colours and combinations; Russian Blues – as their name implies – and last, but by no means least, the Havana Browns, until recently known as Chestnut Browns.

The Abyssinian was first imported from Abyssinia in 1868-9. This charm- ing little cat is a most affectionate and faithful creature. Beautiful to look at, the Normal Abyssinian has a rich brown coat and each hair is banded or ticked with three separate bands of darker colour, except for the hairs on the underbody and inside legs which should be a good deep shade of apricot. Necklaces, bands or bars on the face, body, tail or legs are a serious fault as is a white chin or shirt front. Few Abys have so far been shown without some cream on the chin, although breeders are now producing cats with better, clearer coats. The eyes are green or amber and the general conformation of the Abyssinian's head in my opinion, closely resembles the pictures of the Egyptian cat goddess Bast.

Mention of the cat can be found in manuscripts of a very early date, fossils indicate their existence many, many years before man, and they were known in China 1000 years BC. It is said that the domestic cat was first introduced by the Egyptians and it is known that they venerated cats from Bast, the cat goddess whom they worshipped. Ra, the Sun God often assumed the form of a cat to combat the powers of evil when they took the guise of serpents. Who brought the cat to England is not known, but legend has it that they came to Cornwall with the Phoenicians.

A Red Abyssinian cat has been produced, whose coat does not carry the characteristic ticking of the Normal variety. Abyssinians are nearly always 'one woman' or 'one man' cats whose devotion and obedience to that person is very striking.

The second most popular of the foreign breeds is the Burmese, now available in several colours. These delightful cats, with a character all of their own, have outstandingly beautiful coats. The Browns are particularly renowned for their glossy coats which lie like mahogany coloured satin over their lithe and sinewy bodies. No trace of markings are permitted. The eyes are slanting and oriental in shape and bright yellow in colour. To me their character is the outstanding feature of the Burmese.

Long-haired cats used to be called Persians and a long time ago Angoras. Should you decide you want a kitten for breeding or showing, go to the shows during the summer and

Right, a pair of Rex kittens, one Devon and one Cornish.

autumn and if possible either make your purchase soon after, or order your kitten in advance. Long-haired cats do not breed all the year round hence the necessity of confining your purchase to about four months or so. There are about twenty different coloured long-haired cats, but they should all have the same body conformation, which should be as follows:-

Body – cobby, massive but not coarse.
Head – round, broad with wide space between the ears, which must be small and neat.
Nose – short, cheeks full and muzzle broad.
Eyes – large and round.
Coat – long and flowing.
Tail – short and full

As a general rule you should avoid a kitten whose nose is too flat, as so often this is accompanied by blocked eye ducts, causing weepy eyes, which are uncomfortable for the cat and disfiguring because after a while the tears stain the fur.

They have a quiet and gentle disposition and are less adventurous than some other varieties. Providing they are well groomed each day, for much of their beauty lies in the quality and condition of the coat, they are extremely decorative. Daily grooming is essential for long-haired cats, because unless the coat is kept groomed and untangled, the long hair is a sorry sight. Moreover if the cat attempts to deal with tangled fur by itself it may get furball. The constant washing by kittens and cats means that most of them swallow a certain amount of hair. If a kitten, particularly a short-haired variety, is groomed from an early age, the amount of hair it swallows does it no harm. However, a long-haired cat, or aged cat, which is not groomed regularly, will attempt to deal with all the dead hair itself and will swallow far too much. It becomes congested, hard and indeed, a foreign body, causing pain and discomfort and sometimes needing surgery for its

removal. A weekly dose of liquid paraffin will do much towards keeping older cats reasonably free of obstruction, but nothing replaces regular grooming.

If you want your kitten as a pet, you can easily find one which would be found to have slight faults at a show, but which will be just as adorable and often have more charm and character than the perfect breeding and showing specimen. There are many beautiful varieties from which to choose and it is for the reader to visit shows, read all she can and then make her choice.

Long-haired kittens are full of fun and beauty and when adult, quieter than most of the foreign type cats. To many this is a very definite advantage as it means that when a female comes into season she is far less vocal in her

Below, a maternal British Blue Queen with her newly born kittens. Right, a rather severe-looking Chinchilla kitten.

Left, an Abyssinian cat and her two kittens. The lithe and muscular bodies of the kittens are typical of the breed. Right, a Devon Rex. Below left, a very young Tabby Point Siamese cat and a Foreign White kitten (below right).

Following pages, a Lilac Point Siamese with the correct colouring (top left) and Burmese kittens (below and right).

demand for a mate, which is something to be considered if you live in a flat or any built up area. The following description of a few of the long-haired varieties may help you to choose according to your circumstances.

One of the earliest recognized varieties and a general favourite with many breeders and owners is the Long-haired Blue. It is much sought after by overseas buyers as it is said that the English bred Long-haired Blue is of a very high quality. The coat colour should be an unshaded blue. The standard allows any shade of blue but beware of the paler blue coats as these are subject to damage by strong sunlight. The coat must be long, thick and soft, with a fine, full frill around the head, and the ears small and tufted. The eye colour is

their most striking feature and must be a deep orange, almost copper with no trace of green.

Black Long-hairs were among the first cats to be shown in this country and it would appear there are still only a few of them around compared with other varieties. Perhaps it is because the kittens are less attractive than the kittens of some other varieties such as the Chinchillas or Blue Long-hairs. These black kittens are often brownish grey in colour for the first few months of their life and it is only as they become adult that their full beauty is seen.

As with all Long-hairs daily grooming is absolutely essential. If you intend to show your kitten, or cat, you must never allow the coat to become wet or be exposed to strong sunlight as these elements cause

staining and turn it a rusty colour. As you can see, it would be difficult to keep such a cat and give it full freedom in all weathers if you wished to keep it in first class condition for showing, with the coat retaining its intense black silky colour. Black Long-hairs should have no white hairs in the coat and the hair must be black right through to the skin. One of their most striking features is their glowing orange eye colour and the contrast of such a vivid eye colour with the fine head and ruff of long black silky fur is very beautiful.

It is thought the Long-haired Whites were introduced into France from Persia and as I have mentioned earlier, they were called Angoras. There are three distinct eye colours in the White Long-hairs – the deep orange-eyed, the blue-eyed and the

odd-eyed (one blue, one orange). As with the Black, immaculate grooming is essential. No tinge of yellow must mar the pristine white coat if you wish to show, as purity of colour is of the highest importance. Talcum powder is useful for grooming and the eyes must be kept scrupulously clean and dry to prevent staining around the nose and cheeks. Coats of all three varieties must be long and silky, never woolly. All kittens are born with blue eyes, but around eight weeks of age it is possible to tell into which category the kitten will fall.

Chinchillas are breathtakingly beautiful. They are fairy-like creatures, with a coat of purest white, delicately tipped (or ticked) with black. The kittens are often born

showing tabby markings on legs and tail but in most cases this disappears as the kitten grows and the white undercoat emerges. The Chinchilla body conformation is the same as for all Long-hairs, but the ticking must be even, each hair is tipped with black, giving an impression of sparkling silver. The eyes are also very striking as they are emerald green in colour and rimmed with black, surely the most beautiful of any cat's eyes. Prices for these exquisite kittens are usually high, a consideration most of us have to reckon with, but if you can find and then afford to buy one, your cat will always give you aesthetic pleasure.

Colourpoints, known as Himalayans in the States, were first recognized as a breed in 1955, and are the result of years of selective breeding. Breeders had been trying for some time to achieve a Long-haired Siamese and eventually the basis of our present day Colourpoint was produced and in the hands of a few devoted breeders progressed to the present high stan-

dard. Of these breeders, the Minghchiu prefix is probably the best known over the world for many of these beautiful cats have been exported. The Colourpoint is virtually a Long-haired Siamese, but with the body conformation and the type of the Long-hairs: round broad heads, full cheeks and short nose. They have round, full, blue eyes, cobby body, short, full tails, small, lifted ears and long, thick, silky coat, with points as for the Siamese. The present day Colourpoint is a cat of spectacular and outstanding beauty, which can now be found in many of the Siamese colours.

One of the most recently recognized varieties in this country is the Turkish (Van) cat – sometimes called the swimming cat because it does swim and appears to enjoy the experience. Most cats dislike water, but the Turkish is an exception. This cat really does come from Turkey, and is pure bred, not having been crossed with any other variety. It has been bred in England for about 13 years,

Left, Grey Long-hairs and two beautiful Birman kittens (below).

Above, a family of Colourpoints.
Right, a Short-haired kitten.

reproducing its own kind and demonstrating its purity of breeding. The Turkish cat is not quite the same as the Long-hairs, the head is wedge-shaped, rather than round, the ears are upright and large and not so wide apart. The nose is long, and the eyes are round, amber, and pink rimmed. Their bodies are long and sturdy, the tail is full with faint auburn rings, whilst the beautiful coats are white, long and silky with the same auburn markings. Grooming the Turkish cat is quite a different matter from any other variety and it is strongly recommended that new owners follow the instructions of the breeder before embarking on any form of brushing or combing.

The British Short-hair is a cat which does not require the elaborate grooming of the Long-hair, but should still receive its daily brushing or hand grooming. Its coat, often described as hard, must not be woolly, and should be fine, close-lying and short. These cats have a placid temperament, are ideal with children and do not mind being picked up and handled by almost anyone. They are intelligent and affectionate, and there ought to be more pedigree cats of this variety than there are. Cream, Black, White,

Blue, Red and Blue-Cream, Bi-coloured, Tortoiseshell and the Tortie and White are the colours most regularly seen. Their structure is the same, although they differ in eye colour according to coat pattern. Their heads are round with a short nose and round bold eyes. The ears are small and rounded and the body is well knit, but not long. The tail is thick at the base and fairly short and the feet are round and neat.

The chief characteristic of the Manx cat is its absolute taillessness. In fact there should be a decided hollow where in the ordinary cat, a tail appears. The rump should be round, and the hind legs are longer than the front ones, causing the Manx to have a distinctive hop when running. All colours are recognized for this breed, and they have delightful temperaments but are probably only appreciated fully by those who specialize in breeding them. Unless you have a 'yen' for a cat without a tail, he is not for you. Even for the breeders most interested in producing litters of true tailless cats this variety does not always breed true.

Pet Pride Inc.
No book of this nature is complete

without mention of an American organization – Pet Pride – probably the largest, non-profit-making cat club in the world. With a nationwide membership and interests stretching to Canada and Great Britain, this club does much to prevent the ill treatment and neglect of cats.

The standards required to become a member of Pet Pride are high. The living conditions and hygiene of your cat are inspected, and definite rules are laid down. When membership is granted, a seal of approval is given. This is considered a guarantee to anyone who purchases a kitten, and he in turn must assure the Pet Pride breeder of his integrity and his intention to follow the aims of the Club. A certificate to this effect must be signed by both parties before a sale is completed. Annual membership costs £2 and this goes towards the publication of a regular and informative magazine.

First days with your kitten

It is very possible that you have read about a certain breed or have seen someone else's cat which you like very much, and so have made your decision without going to a breeder or to a show. Consequently you may not know where to find a kitten for yourself. This is what happened to me. Having fallen for the Siamese cats I was impatient to have a kitten as soon as possible, but then I suddenly realized I did not know where to start looking. I rang up various people I knew who had a Siamese cat and asked them where they bought it. Mostly the reply was that the person who bred that particular cat did not breed any more or had moved or had died – anything, but the answer was the same: no kittens. Eventually, I found an advertisement in my local paper, 'phoned the owner and went off to see the kittens. This is not the way to go about buying a kitten, because there are pitfalls about buying haphazardly as I did (although, in point of fact, I was lucky).

My advice to you is to make contact with the breeders who specialize in the variety you prefer and then make your decision. The first thing to decide is whether you want a pet, a show cat or a cat from which to breed. Any pedigree kitten will cost you a certain amount but there are often one or two in a litter of kittens with excellent pedigrees which are not quite perfect and which would not be good for breeding and showing. They of course make excellent pets and if you do not want to breed or show it is unlikely that any technical imperfections in patterning or the shape of the ears will affect you at all. If, however, you feel you would like to breed, you will want one which has the correct characteristics, and this will cost a little more. If you have ambitions to show, then your kitten may cost you a great deal more.

Whatever you decide, do not rush.

Take your time finding your kitten. Meanwhile, buy 'Fur and Feather', the official publication for the Governing Council of the Cat Fancy. You will have to order it from your newsagent as it is seldom to be found on a bookstall. It is published fortnightly and although catering for various animals and birds, many cat breeders put their advertisements in it. You can get the name and address of the Secretary of the GCCF who will give you the names and addresses of secretaries of the various cat clubs.

Then there are cat shows at which you can see all the many different

Curled up asleep in front of the fire – a six-week-old Seal Point Siamese. Kittens usually prefer a box or basket or somewhere cosy and enclosing and this little one looks rather lonely.

breeds and really make up your mind. One of the best for the newcomer is devoted to kittens and neuters – the Kensington Kitten and Neuter Club Show held in London annually, usually in July. Here all types and breeds of pedigree kittens are shown, many of them for sale. The breeders will be helpful if you tell them exactly what you want – pet, breeding or show kitten – and will I am sure do everything possible to help you. If it is a show kitten you want, any of the many judges will give you an honest opinion on a kitten providing you wait until they have finished their judging.

Even though you may see just the kitten you are looking for and long to take it home, never buy a kitten and take it back with you from a show. This may seem hard, even ridiculous, but believe me, it is a wise precaution. Kittens are handled many times at a show. They are also closely confined in a hall with many others, including adult cats. With the best of intentions on the part of the owners, it is fairly certain that one, perhaps several of those present have or are incubating illness. When it is a respiratory illness or an airborne virus it does not need much imagination to appreciate the risk to which all kittens present are exposed. Better to wait another few days than have a sick kitten on your hands. I am afraid there is no foolproof method of buying a kitten

A healthy, bright-eyed Tabby kitten in the pink of condition showing its early ancestry in the tiger-like line of the jaw (right).

and there are no foolproof kittens.

The one factor I would like to stress here for those who want to breed or show is that they should buy the best. Do not rush because 'this one will do'. You may save yourself much time and labour by waiting, either until the right kitten for you appears, or until you can afford the price of a really good one. If the owner of a particular kitten you fancy does not wish to sell, she may be prepared to

repeat the mating and sell you a kitten from the subsequent litter — possibly giving you first choice.

We will suppose you have come to a satisfactory arrangement with a breeder, either to buy a particular kitten or to see some from a litter. In either case you will want to visit the breeder to see the kittens in their home environment. It is important to see the kind of home from which the kitten comes. The size of house does not matter a bit, but cleanliness does. Smell the house, let your nostrils guide you, and this applies to any place where cats are offered for sale. Sick cats and kittens have a definite odour which you do not have to be an expert to recognize. If there is no smell have a good look around. If you hear a sneeze, see a kitten with watery eyes or a dirty nose don't touch it and say a regretful goodbye. Leave just as soon as you can, politeness notwithstanding, for some owners will make excuses about kittens scratching each other's eyes, or the cold weather, or say the kitten has a slight chill. The unsuspecting novice buying his first kitten accepts such excuses, for he knows no better. Buy such a kitten or one from the litter there and the chances are you are buying yourself trouble, and possibly heartbreak. If your eyes, nose and sixth sense tell you all is well, buy your kitten. One warning, do not buy a kitten until its owner has had it inoculated and until it is at least ten weeks old.

All young things are lively and firm to the touch if they are healthy. A kitten's coat should be fluffy and lie straight, as at such an age it will not be sleek or shiny. Its little belly should be firm, not hard; if it is 'ropey' or swollen it is usually a sign of worms. The eyes must be bright, clear and clean — never think of buying a kitten with sticky eyes. The ears should be clean and without smell of any description.

No kitten should be nervous — if the one you like is shy and does not appear to like people or noise, rushing for cover rather than your stockings or your lap — choose another. It is

unnatural for a kitten to want to keep to itself; they are gregarious little animals and like to explore anything or anybody new, and should not rush into hiding to get away from it all.

Should you be unfortunate and should the kitten become ill or die soon after you buy it, and you think you have honestly followed all instructions given by the breeder, contact her, tell her exactly what has happened and how. If she loves her cats and honestly feels you have done all you should, I am sure she will help you. But having read and duly digested these instructions you will be very unlucky if anything goes wrong.

Remember that you get what you pay for – a good price usually buys a good kitten. I once had a most beautiful kitten of very high quality and in spite of repeated requests, I

decided early in her infancy that I could never part with her. She had won many prizes and consequently her fame travelled. When I was approached by a charming Texan lady, who told me she had been commissioned to offer me a very large sum of money for my kitten, I was both surprised and delighted, but still did not want to sell her. She 'phoned me daily from London in an endeavour to change my mind and at last in desperation told me that her friend had authorized her to offer me a blank cheque. Such is fame, though it is not every day that ladies from Texas want to buy cats or kittens!

I am assuming you will have made preparation for the homecoming of the kitten and if it is a pedigree animal, the breeder will have given you a Pedigree Transfer form, Inoculation Certificate and diet sheet. But this

Above, cats always wash their kittens very thoroughly.
Right, a kitten has found his way to a large bowl of milk almost certainly not meant for him.

doesn't always happen, so elsewhere I have, at the risk of repeating what you may already know, given a guide to food and quantities.

When you bring your kitten home, either wrap him warmly in a blanket and carry him in your arms, or put him in the new cat basket you have bought in preparation for this exciting event. It is really better to have a basket, as a frightened kitten may try to escape and you may squeeze him harder than is good for him in your anxiety not to let him go. Here a word of warning – never borrow a basket as it is a good way to introduce disease, and anyway they are quite

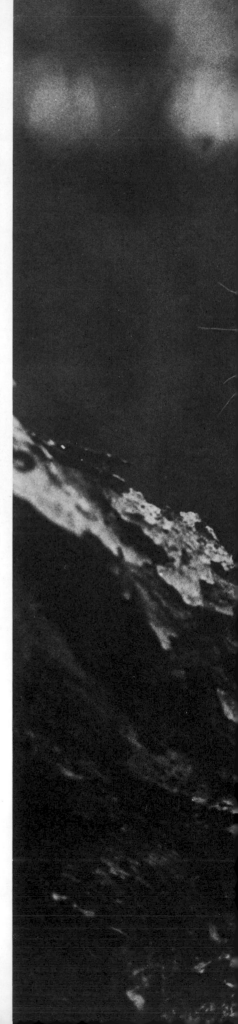

cheap to buy and an essential part of your kitten's equipment. I favour the type which has an inner wire lid, enabling you to see that your kitten is safe and to assure him of your love and attention.

Don't let the rest of the family 'rush' the baby when you arrive home, and watch the children, who, in their excitement, are often noisy and over-whelming. Shut all doors and win-dows so that the kitten can't escape; show him his accessible litter tray and then put him down so that he may explore his new territory. I al-ways keep a new kitten in one room for the first day and then if he shows an adventurous spirit, I allow him full freedom all over the house. If you have your kitten during cold weather, please be careful to put a guard in front of any fire in the room where your kitten might be. He may know nothing about fire and never have seen one before – and heat to him can only be associated with comfort. A startled or excited kitten can so easily jump into a fire with dire results.

This happened to me once. I had brought a strange kitten into the

A Turkish Van kitten exploring the garden in the spring for the first time. Turkish cats are white with auburn rings round the tail and on the face.

house and whilst I was talking to his owner he suddenly, without any warning, made a dash for the fire. His scream of pain and terror echoed through the room as he jumped straight upwards into the chimney in his efforts to escape the burning coals. I immediately covered these with two handy metal shovels and searched upwards for the kitten. It took me ten painful minutes to find him as he had taken refuge on the ledge of a bend in the chimney. He looked a sorry sight when I brought him down, covered in soot, shivering with fright and with four very scor-ched foot pads. I plunged his feet into a liquid paraffin and tannic acid solution, kept for burns, wrapped him in a warm blanket in case of shock and then gave him one teaspoonful of a dilution of brandy, glucose and water. He didn't like it much, but he quickly recovered – then I drank the

52

The typical long face and auburn markings of these unusual Turkish cats can be seen in the mother (left).

rest of the brandy – I considered I had been shocked too! In case you wonder how his coat was cleaned, he had to be bathed in a mild green soft soap without wetting his feet – imagine this – and then sprayed with warm water to rinse out all the lather. He was rubbed as dry as possible and

then kept warm in a room where the fire had a large, kitten-proof guard.

Many people want to know the answer to the vexed question of whether kittens and cats should follow you when you go to bed. There is certainly nothing unhygienic in your pet sleeping on your bed, or even in it; cats and kittens are scrupulously clean all the time and much of their day and night is spent in washing. The first lesson kittens learn from their mother is how to wash them-

selves, and how to do it thoroughly. They will also enjoy washing each other and it is fascinating to watch kittens deliberately washing their brothers and sisters on the back of the neck where they can never reach to wash themselves. A cat's tongue has a rough surface and is specially suited to going to the roots of even a long coat, and sometimes a cat is quite wet after a long and concentrated washing session. They often stop to bite out any mud or loose fur and this is

55

why it is important to brush long-haired cats regularly. Even the wildest alley cat sports a spotless front if it is white, so you need have no fears at all about your pet. However, if you suspect that your kitten has worms then I do not recommend that he sleeps on your bed.

I would like your kitten's first night in his new home to be spent on your bed, but I don't pretend you will have a good night for he will doubtless explore the room, the bed, your ears, hair and eyes and if that doesn't keep you awake his rapturous purrs will not exactly lull you to sleep. Even so, it is worthwhile because nothing reassures a kitten like warmth and human company, especially when all the world has suddenly turned upside down. If you can't face a night with the kitten, make sure he has a small box (kittens and cats hate large ones) with a hot water bottle well wrapped in a warm blanket and he will probably sleep

The Turkish Van family.

well, especially if he has eaten.

The main problem is his litter tray, as many people will, quite understandably, dislike the idea of this coming into a bedroom too. However, it will not be long before he will know where his tray is always kept (please note that it should always be in the same place) and will leave your bed to use it if he has to.

DIET

Before your kitten left the breeder his diet was probably similar to that given below and if you are wise, you will endeavour to carry out these instructions. Many a kitten has had his digestion ruined by new owners who thought they would try out anything they happened to have or who could not be bothered to prepare special dishes. These are the people who, when the kitten is not thriving or has diarrhoea, rush to the 'phone and sometimes accuse the breeder of selling a sickly kitten. Table scraps

An irresistible kitten of no particular breeding cannot decide whether to sleep in the shopping basket or (next page) on the cushions.

are not suitable food for any kitten or cat. I always give written dietary instructions with my kittens and if I get a worried owner on the 'phone, I can almost guarantee that she has substituted an unsuitable food in place of the kitten's normal diet.

Here is the chart on which I have successfully raised hundreds of kittens and if you have not been given a diet sheet, you cannot go far wrong with this one. A kitten should have four meals a day, two milk meals and two protein meals. The first and third meals should be milk and the second and last protein, containing meat, fish, rabbit, chicken, etc. Ordinary cow's milk is not suitable for kittens; wherever I refer to milk I mean the unsweetened, evaporated milk which

is then diluted, two parts milk to one part boiled water.

First meal of the day, which should be given as soon as you get up.

A small saucerful of milk, mixed to a creamy consistency with Farex, or Farlene (I like this one as it has added egg yolk) or baby rice; sometimes I also add a few cornflakes. Twice a week it is a good idea to add half a beaten egg yolk to this meal. I usually make up enough milk mixture in the morning to last for tea time.

The midday meal.
Two dessertspoons of cooked, de-boned rabbit or chicken. I give cooked fish twice weekly, no more. As the kitten gets older, introduce a little raw liver, kidney or heart. Never

make sudden dietary changes, but gradually substitute or add a new food.

Third meal which should be given mid or late afternoon.
Repeat the first meal, but if you have added egg in the morning do not give it again.

Evening meal.
Two dessertspoons of raw minced lean beef. Kittens can tolerate very little fat, although as they grow a certain amount can be included. The beef may be replaced by any other good meat, but it must be raw. Some people give vegetables but I never do, for cats are carnivores and in their natural state eat only raw meat. True, we have domesticated them, but even so, I feel we should feed them as naturally as possible.

Vitamins should be given every day, usually with a milk meal. I give ADEXOL, four drops daily, or ABI-

DEC and also a good pinch of CALCIUM LACTATE or steamed BONE MEAL – not the kind one puts on one's garden, but the sterilized variety, specially prepared for animal feeding. This is the calcium I prefer, because it is the natural bone meal, and anything non-synthetic is, I think, preferable to a man-made preparation. Many people give Cod Liver Oil in winter, but unless this is absolutely fresh it is useless because the vitamin content lessens with age. Halibut Liver Oil is far better and two drops daily during winter as the kitten gets older is a very good idea, so long as he does not dislike the obviously 'fishy' flavour. It can be substituted during winter by ADEXOL which being quite taste-less is often tolerated far better by young things and my kittens are weaned with this additive to their milk.

Increase the amount in the meat meals very gradually adding other

Right, two long-haired Tortoiseshell kittens.

offal to make for variety. Tinned pilchards, sardines, etc., are also excellent and the oil in the latter is most valuable. Mix these with a little brown bread or corn flakes or they may be too rich.

When about five months old the kitten will probably refuse his cereal/milk meal in the afternoon, and three meals a day will be quite enough. The last meal should always be of protein, for this takes longer to digest and the kitten eats nothing again till morning. If your kitten refuses his milk and cereal food, try giving him gravy and cereal. If this fails there is no other

way but to apportion his daily meat ration into three meals. Never leave milk or food on the floor; let him eat eagerly what you give him and then take up the dish, washing it immediately. Fresh water should always be

Left, a Silver Tabby kitten.
Below left, a family of Cream and Orange Long-haired kittens.

Below, a Chinchilla kitten pretending to mouse hunt behind some flowers.

available, as cats always enjoy this. I think I should mention here the fallacy that all cats like and thrive on milk. This is definitely *not* so. Many cannot tolerate the lactose present and will refuse at quite an early age. Many owners then proceed to dilute the milk, thus making it less tolerable than before. The more cream present – like the top of the milk – the better a kitten can tolerate it, for the fat burns up the lactose, thus preventing diarrhoea. This does not apply to all kittens, but if you find yours has a 'loose tummy', try cutting down or

possibly eliminating milk altogether. This usually only happens after about four months of age.

At nine months your kitten will be a cat; and should by this time be having only two meals a day, especially if he is neutered. A young male kept for future stud purposes or a breeding female will, of course, need more, and I hope to deal more fully with these in a later chapter.

One more point. If you have no garden and therefore no access to that most valuable commodity – grass – it is important to provide some for your

cat. Dig up a grass turf, plant it in a pot of earth, water it and leave it where your cat has free access to this essential part of his diet. Grass is an emetic, cleansing the stomach and intestines. If you cannot get turf, grow grass seed in pots in rotation, thus ensuring a never failing supply. Watch the sheer enjoyment of your cat as he chews to be really convinced of whether this is necessary or not.

It is unlikely that he will have been calm enough to eat anything the day you fetched him so next morning he will want his breakfast and here often comes the first battle of wits. The meal will I expect consist of cereal and milk. The kitten may sniff at it, give you a pathetic look and ask 'Where's the rabbit? I don't like this stuff, I have never been given slush before!' Or he may look absolutely disgusted and cast you such a re-

proachful look that you immediately feel guilty of cruelty to animals!

Now is the time to harden your heart as it is often the case that this is the crucial encounter and if you are firm in the beginning you will have no more trouble. If you let a kitten have its own way in the beginning you are letting yourself in for a load of trouble later on with a cat who will only eat extraordinary and usually expensive food! You must persevere, anyway·for a few days, with the milk meal, but it can happen that from the moment you take over a kitten, he will temporarily refuse his milky foods. I think this is often due to the sudden withdrawal of a kitten from the litter, where he has eaten everything because if he didn't his brothers would soon polish off his share.

If such a thing does happen and the

A Blue Point Siamese mousing. This is a beautiful cat with no shading on the back and grace in every line of the lithe and muscular body. Her excitement has made her eyes quite round.

kitten steadfastly refuses milk or milky foods, then make up his breakfast with gravy from his cooked meals. Rabbit, meat or even fish gravy, mixed with a little Farex will usually be acceptable or sometimes a little scrambled egg, or raw egg yolk only. However don't rush to do this, because as I said, it may well be a hoax and if you give in immediately you have lost the battle almost before it began.

You may find that he will just not

be interested in food at all. He may be very excited, rushing from spot to spot, finding life too thrilling to stop for more than a swift mouthful, but you need not worry as he will soon settle down and start to feel hungry. If on the other hand he is shy and rather diffident, a little coaxing may do the trick and he will respond gratefully to your overtures, for he will be feeling very lonely. If you have been given a diet sheet, stick to it and you cannot go far wrong. Whatever you do, don't substitute something 'a little more tasty' just to tempt him. For one thing this tasty morsel could upset him if he is unused to it, and for another you are starting a habit which any kitten will take the opportunity to perpetuate and which, if persisted in, will turn him from a good unfussy kitten into a finicky cat. Don't get neurotic

about the eating habits of your kitten. If he is healthy he will eat all you give him within a few hours. If he doesn't, contact your breeder, for she will want to know. Always pick up his plate after feeding. A kitten should polish off his food within ten minutes and if he leaves bits and pieces pick them up and cook them so that they may safely be fed at the next meal.

I always tell the buyers of my kittens that providing they follow my written instructions I consider myself fully responsible for the kitten for the first ten days, after which I expect to be informed if a kitten isn't settling, for I would far sooner have him back than leave him with his new owner to 'muddle through'.

By lunch time the kitten will be well on the way to becoming settled. Memories of his earlier life will be

fading and the speed at which this happens is usually dependent upon his new owner – or owners. Please do not overfeed your kitten. He needs approximately one to one and a half ounces of protein to every pound he weighs. So if he weighs four pounds, he will need about four to five ounces of meat, fish or rabbit a day, divided into two meals; as well as his milk, egg and cereal food. It is difficult to be tough when he says he is starving – which he no doubt will do very often – he is just plain greedy, if he is healthy.

At this point I would like to speak of something about which I feel strongly. If you can afford to feed a pair of kittens, and by this I mean giving to two exactly the same good quality food as you would to one, then please decide to buy a pair. It is

good fresh smell if renewed frequently and the more often this is done, the better for the kitten and his owner. Whilst earth is dirty and often difficult to obtain, peat on the other hand is clean but has certain disadvantages which I will explain. However, providing the medium in the tray is kept fresh, young kittens will use it, for they are remarkably undemanding.

Many cats and kittens live in flats, in which case it may be impossible to obtain shavings or earth and to dispose of them. In this event, one of the prepared litters is more convenient.

People will often use peat which they then place on their garden to rot down. This is an extremely dangerous practice for if your pet should harbour such parasites as worms, the larvae will be passed out in the litter into the garden. As it takes up to two years for some larvae to be destroyed you must not put the contents of a litter tray anywhere near your vegetables. If you must use peat, put it in a little-used part of the garden for two years or burn it. However, anyone with a garden should not have to make use of a litter tray in any case, as a kitten will either already know about gardens from his first home, or even if he has only lived in a flat he will very quickly explore and enjoy a garden.

Nearly all kittens are naturally house trained. This is the wonderful difference between kittens and puppies. Kittens virtually train themselves and I can almost guarantee that once you show your tiny pet where to find his sanitary tray, he will never give you cause to call him dirty. I find a kitten will usually use his tray soon after a meal. Therefore, if he has a clean one after breakfast, he will often not need it changed until evening. Kittens and cats hate using dirty boxes and if mistakes occur, it is usually because he doesn't like his soiled litter and can you blame him?

Litter trays must always go into the same spot, with one exception, which I will explain later, for although an older kitten will eventually find his tray wherever it is, a new one may be nervous and have left himself short of time in which to make a protracted search.

so rewarding having two kittens that you will never regret your possible extravagance. Have you ever seen two kittens playing together? They are the best time wasters I know. Feeding two is easier because appetites are better, with competition they will never be lonely, and they will take no time at all to settle into a new place. Later on when you are away from home there will be no forlorn and pathetic little loner anxiously awaiting your return. This does not mean that two kittens will not give you as much affection as one would, but that their dependence upon you is not painfully obvious. I know of two cats, sisters, who are devoted to each other and who have never been separated, but who are also equally devoted to their owners, following them around and joining in every activity they can. When their owners return after leaving the house empty, the cats are always waiting for them to come home, but there are two of them to keep the vigil. The chances are that they will be thoroughly annoyed with their owners for going away in the first place rather than pathetically glad to see them again, as a solitary cat would be. I can see absolutely no reasons against having a pair of kittens if you can afford to feed them in the right way.

It is important to have an efficient and suitable litter tray. A good plastic baby bath or square bowl not less than 14 inches by 12 inches and about 5 inches deep is the best thing for the purpose. I find wood shavings (not sawdust, which can damage a kitten's eyes) an ideal medium. You only need a couple of large handfuls each time. Shavings are absorbent and easily burnt and they have a

Above, learning to beg at an early age. Right, the Turkish Van cat deals with her kitten's dirty face.

Life with your kitten

No one wants a home ruined by the cat's claws, and with a little basic training I believe it is not a necessary evil if one has a cat. All kittens will run up curtains and swing on the backs of chairs – it is for you to inform your pet that although you appreciate his high spirits, he has to channel his antics into more acceptable games. I do not honestly think you can prevent a tiny kitten from exploring the curtains, chair bottoms and the stair carpet, but as he grows older, so will the amount of damage he inflicts increase, so make him a scratching post. I have heard people say their cats will not use them, but I think this is because the kitten is not introduced early enough to this vital piece of equipment.

A scratching post must have a fairly heavy base, approximately 18 inches by 18 inches in the centre of which is nailed or screwed a stout pole. Cover the pole with a piece of old carpeting, tacking it firmly down. Rub over the carpet surface with a little dried cat-mint – bought from most pet stores – and then encourage your kitten to scratch. I believe the catmint, which is quite irresistible to all cats, first attracts them and then they will realize that there is a nice piece of

carpet. If you regard the kitten scratching anywhere else with disfavour and treat him to a stern 'No' he may learn to resist the temptation of other carpets, chairs and curtains, which he will undoubtedly prefer, and only use his post. Cats are extremely consistent. They will invariably go for the same chair or the same area of carpet, so get your kitten used to his scratching block early, and he will always use it. (See page 74.)

Train your kitten from the start to travel in a car with you. Buy him a collar (elasticated) or harness and lead and let him become accustomed to these first. Then take him in the car, watching carefully to see that he does not take fright, and talking reassuringly to him during the journey. If he learns about the noise and motion in his early days he will probably become a seasoned traveller.

If you have only one kitten he will need toys with which to play. These will not only amuse him but will help

Two Abyssinian kittens playing and fighting together. It is interesting that the kitten underneath is instinctively attacking his brother in exactly the same way that he will later attack and kill a rabbit.

to develop his body. It will also give his owners immense pleasure to watch the contortions of this small creature as he tosses his toy high into the air or carries it, growling fiercely, under chairs and tables. He can, even at such an early age, pretend his mouse is alive, tuck it under a mat and apparently, with all the guile of an old stager, turn his back on it. The next moment he leaps into the air, scrabbles under the edge of the rug with all four feet and emerges triumphant with his prey. Many kittens are incredibly graceful and can perform wonderful 'ballets' as they play. They quickly appreciate an audience and will dance with ever-increasing complexity and skill if they know that you are watching. As they grow older they

will become aware of their dignity, but many cats will continue to play until middle-aged if they have been given suitable toys at an early age.

I never give my kittens plastic or rubber toys – these are dangerous and rather boring. Kittens prefer something that will change shape, and something made of stuff that their claws can catch hold of. Kittens are imaginative creatures and a piece of rag, tightly sewn into a two inch sausage shape will for him assume the form of an unknown enemy to be tossed and trampled.

I am sure you will find all the most successful toys will either be made by you or even discovered by the kitten himself by accident. Paper and string, stuffed felt toys and animals, rag

Above, Siamese are remarkably quick and graceful players – and this kitten is starting young.

Right, Ginger and white kitten. Following pages, Long-haired Whites.

balls and wool are all acceptable, though it rather depends on whether you have a graceful kitten which likes to use his toy as an excuse to dance and fly through the air or whether you have a kitten with strong hunting and destructive instincts. I find an excellent all-purpose toy is a pipe cleaner spider. Take three pipe cleaners, cross them at the centre and

make a star shape. Bind them in the centre with wool, turn down the 'legs' one third and you have a spider. This toy, especially if made with bright wool, will give your kitten endless pleasure, as it is light enough to toss and the pipe cleaner legs will stand up to tremendous punishment without breaking and endangering the kitten. I also make catnip balls – small pieces of linen or cotton filled with dry catnip and sewn into balls about the size of a table tennis ball. Again they are light, cheap and renewable.

One of the ways to amuse any kitten, or kittens, is with a medium-sized cardboard box. Turn it upside down and cut a hole three inches by three inches in three out of the four sides. This makes a little house of sorts and one which will give endless hours of pleasure to you and the kitten. Another excellent thing for kittens to hide in and play with is a large paper bag, though they find it so much fun that the bag doesn't last more than an hour or two!

Whilst I am on the subject of cardboard boxes – try putting one over the sanitary tray, with only a 'front door' opening. You can paint it or make it of wood, paper it with wallpaper, decorate it – in fact there are endless ways of hiding a litter tray, and I believe the cats like the privacy such a cover gives.

When the kitten has been with you for a week or so, it is a good idea to worm him. You will probably wonder why, particularly if he has not even been outside, but kittens and puppies are often born with worms ingested from the mother. Although there are several types of worm to which the cat can become host, I shall deal only with the two most common.

Round worms are very common in kittens and young cats. The signs are a 'pot belly' or extreme thinness, poor 'staring' coat, variable appetite, sometimes ravenous, often the reverse, and occasionally persistent diarrhoea.

Right, kitten and ping pong ball. Left, non-pedigree and pedigree . . . a fluffy black and white kitten (above) and a normal Abyssinian kitten well camouflaged against the flowerbed.

Ask your vet to give you some tablets for your kitten. He will quite likely give you Piperazine, harmless to the kitten and necessitating no starvation before treatment. However these tablets are relative to the weight of the cat, so you may have to weigh your kitten and then divide up the pill accordingly. Give your kitten his breakfast (milk and cereal) and about two hours later pick him up and place him on the table. If you have crushed the pill into powder take a teaspoon and scoop the powder on to the back of the spoon handle. Take the kitten by the scruff of his neck, and if you have anyone to help you ask them to hold his front paws and, at the same time, open his mouth. As soon as this is done, place the spoon handle quickly in his mouth, getting it well in and then hold his jaws together for a moment or two, at the same time releasing his

Above, a really good scratching post made of heavy wood and stout carpet. This kitten also has a stuffed mouse. Right, yet another plaything.

neck until he has swallowed. Immediately after offer him a little undiluted evaporated milk (for which most kittens would sell their souls) to take away any bitter taste. The kitten will

usually use his box within two hours, and the contents must then be immediately burnt. This treatment kills the worms but not the eggs laid by them, so treatment must be repeated ten to fourteen days later. In one week, the improvement in your kitten will be phenomenal. His coat will shine, he will be more lively and his growth rate will increase enormously. After the second dosing, you have really given him a head start in life.

I believe in worming kittens every three months for round worms, as I think these parasites are devitalizing to such an extent that they lower a kitten's resistance and make him subject to further diseases. Often parasites carry bacterial infections which make it imperative to rid your kittens of these unwanted guests. Remember that a well fed, healthy kitten has a natural defence which repels parasites like round worms.

The Tape worm is so called because the worm looks rather like a flat piece of tape. It appears mostly in young adult cats, giving them much the same symptoms as do round worms. Often the worm's presence is confirmed by the small segments adhering to the cat in the vicinity of the anus. The eggs of the tape worm fall from an infected cat to the ground where they dry. They are then picked up by fleas and after various changes

Left, 'Why won't you play?'. An Abyssinian kitten hugs his mother in the attempt to get her attention.

Above, cats and kittens love catmint and this young cat is rolling in ecstacy on a toy mouse stuffed with dried catmint.

the flea finds a fresh host in another cat who will swallow it when washing himself, and the whole process is complete. Tape worms are difficult to eradicate and the simple answer is – no fleas, no tape worms. The treatment and removal of tape worm is best discussed with your veterinary

surgeon, who will be fully conversant with the latest form of treatment.

Most people know that if you have a puppy, one of the things you must do when he is twelve weeks old is to have him inoculated against distemper and hard pad. A kitten is in exactly the same need of protection against a killer disease called *Panleucopenia*, otherwise known as Feline Infectious Enteritis. If you have bought a pedigree kitten, he or she is almost certain to have been inoculated. Although most vets have posters in their waiting rooms describing this disease, it seems that many cat owners are unaware of its existence. There appears to be little

publicity, although I cannot think why because your pet is just as precious be he a puppy or a kitten, and Feline Infectious Enteritis is 95% fatal. Few kittens survive once they are infected, and a cat may pick it up at any age. Therefore, as soon as the kitten is ten weeks old, take him to your vet for an inoculation against F I E. If you ask your vet for this injection he will at once know what you mean and be delighted to give it. With the inoculation the vet will fill in a certificate giving details of your kitten, the date of inoculation and the number of the vaccine given. It is wise to keep this certificate because if you ever want to leave your cat or kitten in a boarding cattery, you must give evidence that your cat has been inoculated. If a cattery is not particular about this it cannot be a good one. Although this will not guarantee that your kitten may never pick up the disease, he will certainly stand a very good chance of recovery if he has been inoculated.

There are several vaccines now on the market – the one I favour is a *live* vaccine, given at ten weeks, in only one injection. This will protect him for three years, after which he will need a 'booster', to keep up his immunity. Do not mistake 'Cat Flu' for F I E. Many owners believe the injection which is sometimes given if a cat has a cold or 'flu is the same thing, but it quite definitely is not. You will be given a certificate from your vet with an F I E inoculation but not with a cold or 'flu injection.

There is absolutely no reason for a kitten to have fleas. It is easy to eliminate them, even in summertime, if your pet is unfortunate enough to bring them into your home. Fleas are the hosts to tape worms and can cause anaemia, therefore do try to get rid of them as they cause more pain and poor health than any other sickness. They will keep your pet from eating and sleeping properly, and in most cases the kitten will tire himself out at night scratching. Buy a good flea powder, one which does not contain DDT, and a good flea comb, sold by most chemists. Dust your kitten all over with the powder, being particularly careful not to get any near his eyes. Pop him into a large polythene bag up to the neck and hold him firmly on your lap for about ten minutes or longer if you can. By that time the fleas will have dropped off into the bag, so that when you take him out, all you need to do is comb him thoroughly with the flea comb, thus removing the powder and any remaining fleas. Burn the polythene bag. A run through with the comb once a day will keep him free from vermin and at the same time help his grooming.

Examine your kitten's ears. They should appear perfectly clean if your kitten has come from a good home. If, however, they appear to have rather dark wax or dirt inside put a little cotton wool around an orange stick, dip lightly into olive oil and gently wipe round the crevices, being extremely careful not to penetrate too deeply. You may have noticed your kitten scratching his ears or rubbing his head along the floor, and if this is accompanied by the dark wax inside the ears the kitten needs more specialized treatment, and a prompt visit to your vet is indicated. It usually means your kitten has parasites which can lower the general condition of the kitten in much the same way as fleas, and are extremely contagious.

All kittens should get daily grooming if possible. This entails inspecting the ears, swabbing the eyes gently with a little cotton wool and grooming the coat. The earlier he gets used to this the more he will tolerate it and later he will probably thoroughly enjoy the routine. There are many

A Colourpoint kitten with two ideal toys – a fir cone and a ball of paper.

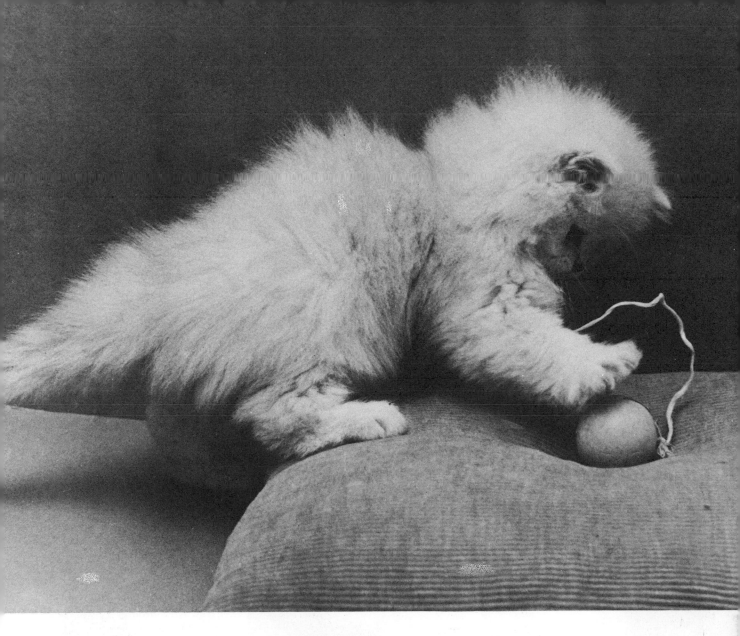

A bundle of fluff about to start a game with a ball and string. Long-haired kittens are not so clever and graceful when they play as the Foreign type cats, but can be very endearing.

methods of grooming. Some people use a soft brush and a comb and if you have a long-haired kitten a brush is the best thing to use. Others use a silk cloth or chamois leather. I have a method for short-haired cats which I have used satisfactorily for years! I take a clean rubber glove, dampen it, almost dry it on a cloth and then stroke in long sweeps from the head to the tail. I repeat this process on the legs, round the eyes in gentle movements and then do again the flanks, back and tail. It is quite astonishing how much dead hair comes away with the glove. A word of caution here, don't pull the hair, stroke firmly and

gently. I then finish off with a soft silk scarf and I find this a perfect method of grooming.

I would advise owners of short-haired kittens to be wary of hard brushing after my experiences of brushing a very beautiful Blue Point Siamese with the true glacial coat. I intended to show him when he would be old enough, so I started his daily sessions when he was quite tiny, using a brush and occasionally a comb so that he should get the feel of them. These sessions went on through the early weeks of his life, through the moulting of the baby coat and well into his seventh month. A few weeks before his first show I noticed a dark, coarse streak of hair appearing down his back, from neck to tail. I asked an experienced judge what it could be and when she told me I had over-groomed him, or rather that I had been too enthusiastic with the brush, I threw the offending article away

and never used one again on a short-haired cat.

Grooming long-haired kittens is vitally important because as I have already mentioned there is the danger of the cat swallowing furballs. They should be brushed in the opposite way to a smooth-coated animal, as a long-hair needs to sport his ruff and must never be smoothed down. It is also essential that he is well brushed and combed around his back legs and tail, as it is here that the knots will accumulate most quickly. Unless daily attention is given to his coat the fur will get matted to such an extent that only scissors can remove the lumps and this leaves a very untidy, ragged effect, with lumps of cut hair.

Finally it is essential to watch the claws as I once learnt when a beautiful blue long-haired cat came to stay with me. I gave him the usual examination, found him well and reasonably groomed and was thank-

79

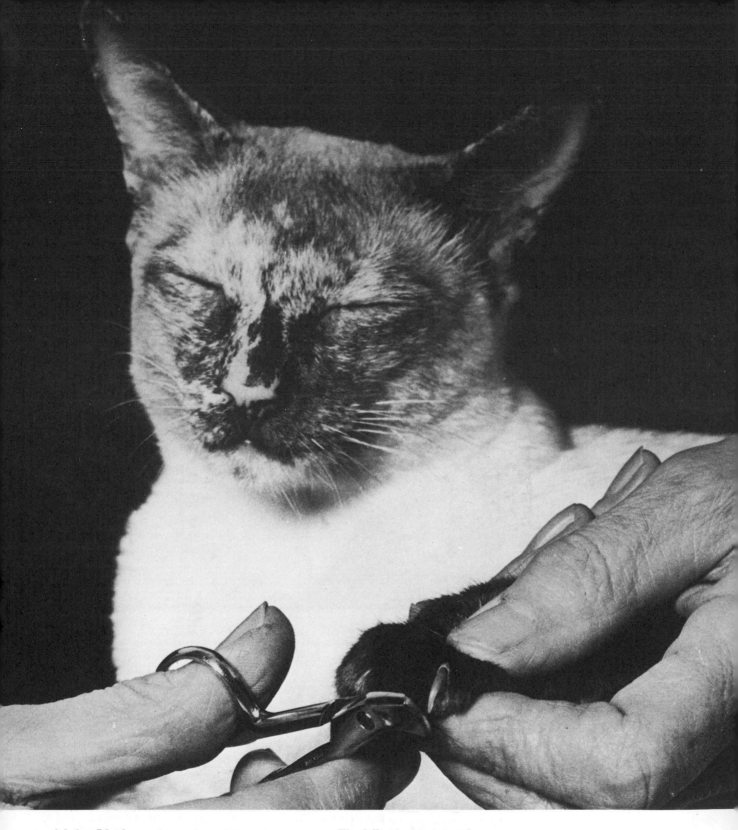

ful that I had a cat in good condition. The first 24 hours he stayed quietly in his box, but soon his confidence grew and he came out into his garden, jumped upon his shelf and decided we were reasonable humans. The next day we took advantage of these overtures and started his daily grooming, which, I am glad to say, he tolerated with only the occasional flick of his tail when I became a bit insistent about the small knots on his hind-

quarters. The following morning there were spots of blood on the floor and shelf in his house and I promptly examined his ears, nose, and body for wounds. It was not until I turned him upside down to look at his tummy that I saw what was wrong. The claws on his back feet had, under cover of the long foot hairs, grown longer and longer until one of them had curled under and actually penetrated the pad, causing the wound which was

Above, sometimes a cat's claws can grow too long and be an irritation, so they should be gently clipped – this Tortie Point Siamese has his eyes shut showing he really quite enjoys it.

Right, a young Abyssinian cat.

Above, a Silver Tabby kitten in his basket. These are spectacular cats with beautifully marked coats.

Left, a Tabby kitten.

now issuing blood and pus. I immediately called in my vet and although all was well in the end it meant surgery to extricate the claw.

The cat owner who has a vet who loves cats is fortunate indeed, for he is a treasure beyond price. If you have breeding ambitions, a good vet with a knowledge of cats is an essential part of your programme, for you will not get very far without him. Until recently little has been known about feline diseases, and there are many vets who prefer dealing with dogs or large animals. It is, therefore, well worth while searching for one in your area who will be sympathetic and whom you can trust. Incidentally,

you will find one much more easily if you let him know that he can also trust you not to panic.

A vet has a limited time for home visiting and dislikes unnecessary calls upon his precious time. As soon as he learns you do not panic he will probably come willingly when you ask him to and would far sooner be told of any symptoms that worry you than be faced with a half-dead kitten. If you have several cats or kittens

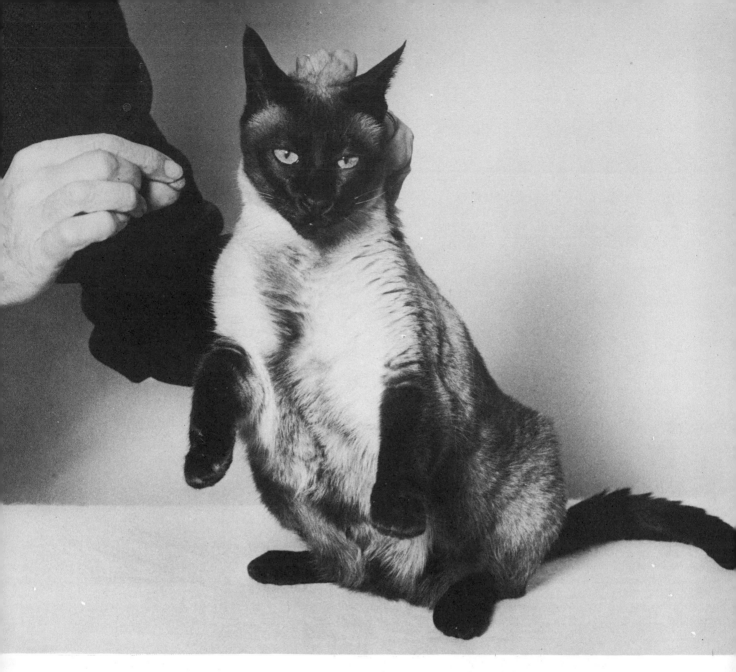

some vets even like to arrange a periodical call just to look all of them over.

Much has been written about cat diseases and they can sound pretty overwhelming. I have no intention of describing all the various illnesses, as this is for professionals to do, but like most things in life a little common sense, plus some guidance, will help you to recognize when expert attention should be sought.

Kittens are, by and large, healthy little creatures. Their pulse rate is 90–100, their normal temperature 101°–102°F so don't panic if they appear to be hot or breathing quickly – they will certainly breathe a good deal faster than you!

The main points to watch are the following:

If a kitten misses a meal, but seems well and lively, don't worry. If he misses two, watch carefully, because he may have a digestive upset. Has he had more fat than usual, stolen extra food, or had his head in the milk jug? Any of these indiscretions will eventually give him a 'loose' tummy but he will be lively and playful. Should he, however, appear lethargic, wanting only to stay in his box and quite disinclined to play, he may have rather more than a digestive disturbance so take him quickly to your vet.

Coughs, sneezes, running of eyes or nose, or both, are conditions that need expert advice. Please don't delay, because if you do you make recovery more difficult for your kitten and certainly do not help your vet.

Accidents, falls, burns, bites, etc, need not be fatal though they can

The three stages of giving your kitten or cat a pill. Above, lift the cat by the scruff of the neck, bringing the front feet off the ground. This makes the cat helpless, though if necessary get someone else to hold the front feet. Right, open the cat's mouth and push the pill well down its throat from the side of the mouth where your finger will be safe from the teeth.

produce shock and this, unless you are very experienced, requires immediate attention.

Raised haws are the third and inner eye lids, not usually seen in a healthy kitten, and are a sign that all is not well. If the kitten also has a rough and 'staring' coat, seek professional assistance.

All these signs are easy to see. If

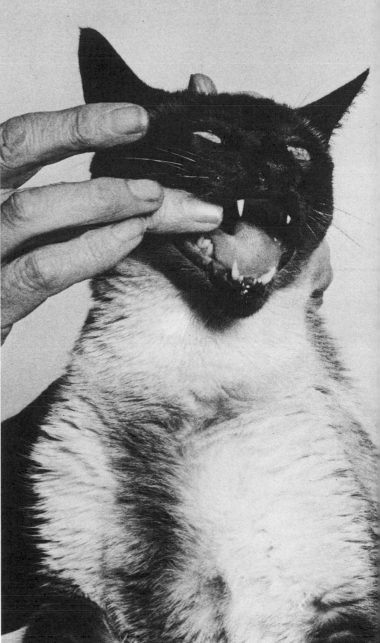

serious illness is pending, your kitten's behaviour will quickly convey his distress, for a lively kitten is seldom a sick one.

Cats are happier when they have a garden to go out in and when there is no litter tray with which to bother, but this does not mean that flat dwellers cannot keep cats. Many older people, for instance, prefer a kitten or a cat to a dog because they are invariably house trained, don't need exercising and are less expensive to feed. However, air and some exercise is a problem as a kitten cannot live inside the whole time. I have a friend, living in London, who has three cats. She works all day but as soon as she gets up in the morning, she opens the door of her upper storey flat and away go her cats. She watches whilst they negotiate the plank ladder she has

erected as far as an upper ledge. They leap this with agility, and disappear over London's roof tops. Half an hour or so later they troop back, coming in through an open window, having had their morning exercise. This procedure is repeated when she returns home in the evening. In fifteen years, she tells me, there has been only one accident when a little female with poor eye sight lost her footing and fell twenty feet to a ledge below. The cat was injured, but not badly, and she did not feel that this accident justified her in curtailing the cats from going off, when so many of her successive cats had taken their exercise this way without mishap.

Accidents can happen in the most organized homes, particularly when the kittens are young. I have many times heard of kittens being scalded,

and it can happen much more easily than you might think. A kettle filled too full and put to boil with the spout pointing outwards, can boil over on to a kitten playing on the floor nearby. Likewise a saucepan left boiling without a lid can be dangerous. An inquisitive kitten seeing a handle sticking out may try to jump up and the saucepan will overturn. Please do see that all handles and spouts are turned so that they do not overhang the top of your cooker. Oil stoves and open fires of any kind are lethal where there are active animals. I recently saw a cat house burned to the ground because a cat knocked over an unprotected oil burner. Backing a car out of the garage is another thing which can lead to tragedy. If you have ever seen a kitten run over by a reversing car, you will never again start up before

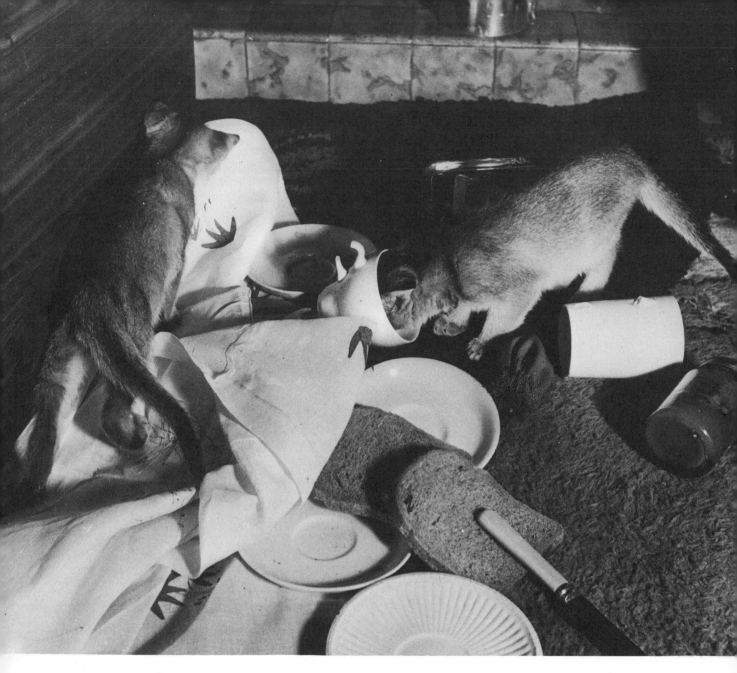

making quite sure that no animal is within reach.

Finally do watch drawers and cupboards and anything that opens and shuts. Kittens are very clever at getting into unexpected places. I once had a very unusual and unnerving experience. It was during a miserable winter's day that I decided to re-upholster a small chair. Turning it upside down I stripped off the old webbing, canvas and lining and in a short time was completely absorbed in my job.

I stopped midday to feed a litter of kittens I had with me and having picked up the dishes, went back to the upholstering. I worked steadily right through the afternoon, with all the kittens, having wakened from their after-lunch sleep, giving me a helping hand. I fixed the webbing, securely

nailed the canvas and turned the chair upon its feet, well satisfied with what I considered a good job.

By this time it was past tea time for the kittens, so I rushed to prepare their milk and cereal and as I always give each kitten its own individual dish, I realized as I placed them on the floor that I had one over – only six kittens and seven plates! I searched everywhere, my family arrived home and they joined me, but there was no number seven.

Suddenly one of my daughters said, 'I suppose you haven't sewn him into the chair?' We tore off the lining, then the webbing (how strongly I had nailed them into place) and when all was stripped away, there in the left hand corner was one fat little bundle curled up asleep! So don't upholster furniture with kittens around.

Kittens on the rampage . . . knitting is fascinating (the needles can be dangerous, so do not leave them around), as indeed are daffodils. But the first destructive game has been to knock the tea table over in front of the hearth.

You always have to watch anything that a kitten might find his way into – I heard of one kitten going to the laundry one morning. The bundle of clothes had been tied up and left in a heap on the floor, the kitten had investigated and found this a most comfortable and exciting new bed, curled up and gone sound asleep. He consequently was carried off to be 'washed' and was only just found in time.

A Burmese kitten flying through the air in pursuit of a bunch of feathers.

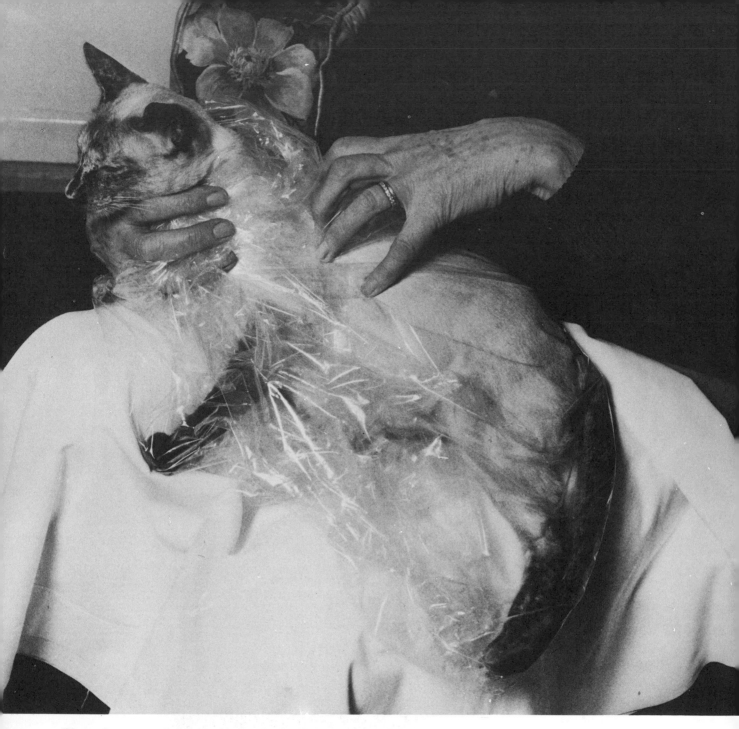

Please be very careful, especially when there are children in the house, that you neither shut your kitten's tail in a door, nor tread on him. Watch out for the kitten tendency to make a concerted rush towards you whenever you enter their room, and leave yourself one free hand, particularly if you are carrying anything.

Here are some 'don'ts'.

Don't leave your refrigerator door open and unattended – kittens are inquisitive especially of places where food is kept.

Don't allow your unattended kitten outside in wet weather. He must be old enough to get inside again whenever he feels chilly and a tiny kitten can so often slip out without

one's knowledge and then be shut out.

Don't put your cat out at night if he cannot get in again. This is a barbaric practice.

Don't wash your kitten's dishes with your own. Although cats are one of nature's cleanest animals, it is far more hygienic to wash his dish under hot running water after you have done your own.

Don't allow your kitten to drink out of a milk jug. No one likes to think of a kitten's tongue coming into contact with one's own food.

Don't leave empty tins lying around. Your kitten may get his head stuck. If you do have empty tins, flatten them!

Don't use weedkillers where your

Above, an excellent method of ridding a cat of fleas (see page 78).
Right, a Long-haired Silver Tabby.

kitten or cat has access. These, when licked from his feet, can cause him grave illness and possibly death. If you must use a weed killer, keep your cat confined until you are certain no trace remains.

Don't leave rubber bands where your kitten can find them – they can get lodged in the intestines.

Don't allow kittens or cats to play with plastic bags as these can prove lethal. Paper is much more amusing and anyway, it rustles!

BREEDING AND REARING

If you have not had your kitten or kittens spayed you may want to breed seriously and provide your cat with a male of your own choosing, and it is a good idea to be as well prepared as you can. It is possible for a kitten to come into season at the early age of four months, but normally the first season is not until the cat is adult and about nine to twelve months old. Several things contribute to oestrus in a cat (known as 'calling'), sunlight being one of the most important. For some reason, light affects the breeding cycle of most animals and the cat is no exception! If you have a pedigree queen you will be anxious to know when she is about to call for the first time. There will be absolutely no doubt about it when she starts her call but you must recognize the earliest symptoms in time to keep her safely shut away from eager males, all anxious to show her the path of love and with whom she will be most eager to tread that path.

There is absolutely no reticence about a calling queen – she wants love and she calls to anyone prepared to listen, be he a mangy farm Tom or a feline Don Juan, and she will escape if she possibly can. It is only the Siamese who have such a violent way of calling; you will never forget the sound once you have heard it. Other breeds, even some of the foreign type cats, have a far quieter way of announcing their desires to the world at large, whilst the Long-hairs and the British cats are so restrained that unless you watch them carefully you may not realize what is happening. I shall describe what happens if you have a Siamese queen, as they are the most

THE KITTENS

A Tortoiseshell cat feeding her litter, which is rather remarkable in that every kitten is white.

dramatic of all calling cats.

About two days before she utters any sound, you will probably see a suitor or two around – I hope for your sake not more. This may puzzle you, as your cat is apparently completely indifferent and utterly disinterested, and there is no reason for this invasion. Next day, she will be very much more affectionate than usual, rubbing herself around the table and chair legs, or any surface within reach, gently rolling on her back and frequently washing her tail end. She will appear to have fallen violently in love with you and will follow you around, rolling and capering for your benefit. A few hours later, your ears will be

assaulted by the most extraordinary sound, rather like a cross between a wailing baby, a barking dog, and a cry of anguish and you will have no doubt that your young cat is calling. As soon as you hear this sound put her under lock and key. Shut every window and block up the fireplace – for if she is able to escape, I assure you she will.

The next days and possibly nights are going to be difficult for you until you get used to both the noise and her precocious behaviour. She will lose her appetite for food as her desire for a mate increases. If one is going to mate a female the ideal time is when she is 'treading'; however, no cat

should be mated on her first call and it is better to wait until her second call, which usually occurs three weeks later. As each call lasts approximately eight days, you can now understand why it is important to decide what you intend to do about the cat's future when she is still a kitten.

People often buy a pedigree female kitten with the strict intention of spaying her and keeping her simply as a pet. In this case they tell the breeder and she sells them a kitten which for several reasons is more suitable as a pet than as a breeding queen. However, somehow the owners never get around to having the kitten spayed; the kitten grows to adulthood and the

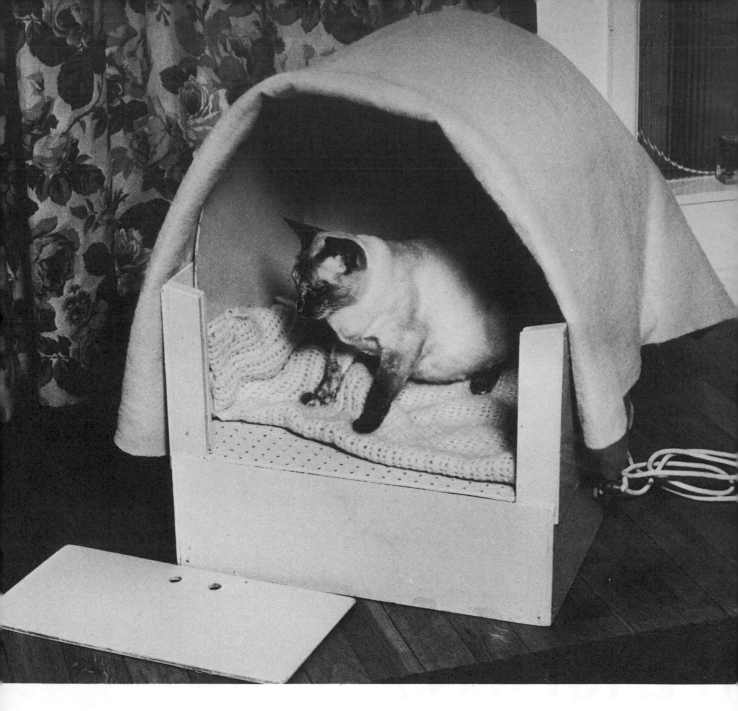

owner decides it would be good for her to have just one litter and then have her operated on. The disadvantage of this plan is that the cat is forever after only interested in babies – her single-minded devotion to you has gone and although you may spay her after this one litter, it is my personal opinion that the queen is never so fully settled as if she had been spayed earlier, so you may be disappointed. On the other hand, your first litter may prove such a success that you will be tempted to go on breeding and perhaps show one of the kittens.

If you honestly have such an idea at the back of your mind – buy a female suitable for breeding, in other words, the best you can afford, as I have already said. Breeding is a serious business, only the healthiest and finest specimens should be used for this purpose, although the temptation to have one litter only is very great and quite understandable.

Females often become very cunning after one or two planned litters and decide they will choose their own mate. Most breeders have had queens who will show absolutely no sign of a call. An unsuspecting owner lets her out and the queen is away to find her own husband. As soon as you discover this the only thing you can do is sit back and await firstly her return in full cry, thin and exhausted, and then later a motley selection of adorable and beautiful kittens.

I am assuming you have coped with your female's first call and that

The box especially designed by Marjorie Hudson as a suitable place for her cats to have their kittens. The picture above shows the flap down and a blanket put over the top and back. The picture right shows the flap up (see page 106). Notice that this Tortie Point is pregnant.

Right, a Tabby kitten photographed when only a few hours old.

A British Blue Queen kneading with
pleasure as she settles down after
giving birth to her kittens.

*The same British Blue family; the
kittens are about two days old.*

*Right, a Chocolate Point Siamese
Queen, belonging to Marjorie
Hudson, nursing her kittens. They ar
four days old and as yet it is quite
impossible to tell whether the kittens
will be Chocolate or Seal Point.*

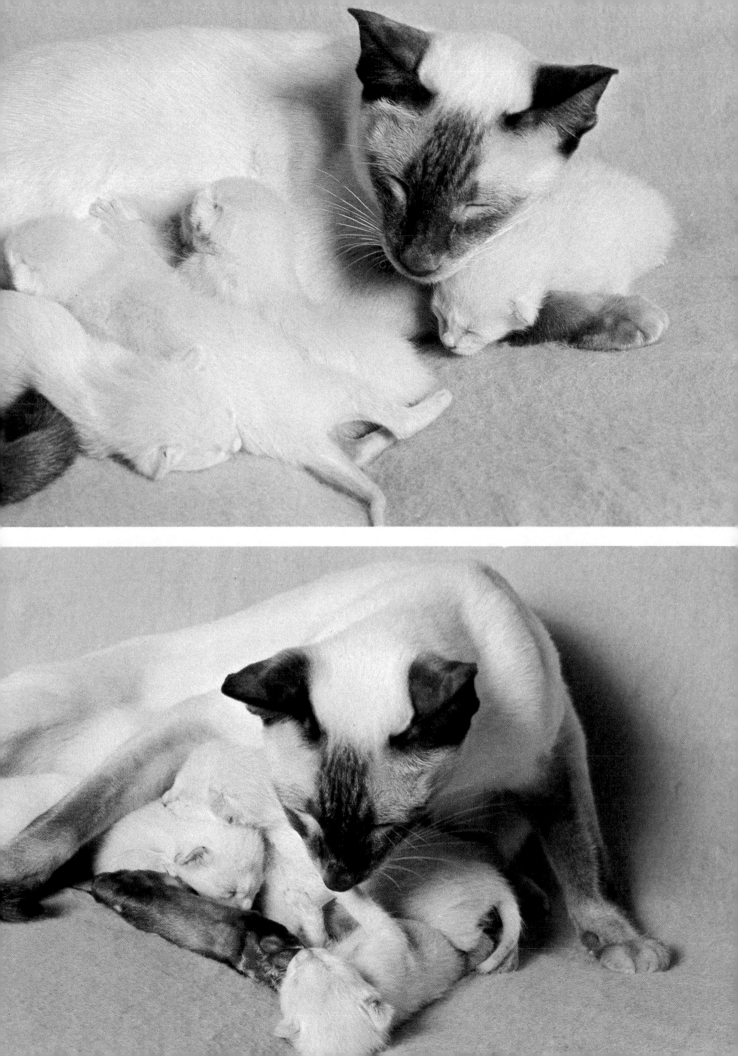

Above, the same Siamese family at four and a half weeks.

Below, two Red Point Siamese kittens aged six months with their mother.

Right, a Silver Tabby kitten stealing the top of the milk.

you have decided to allow her to have a pedigree litter. If you have not already done so, you must start to think of a suitable mate for her – known as a stud – and in doing this I think a novice breeder needs some advice. An obvious person to help you is the breeder from whom your kitten came. She may say she would like to see your cat, thus enabling her to assess her good and bad points, for obviously she will recommend a stud which will help to correct your queen's weaknesses.

If, for some reason, this course of action is not possible, try to visit a cat show and see for yourself the males which are at public stud. If you see no cat that appeals to you, ask advice from any owner or breeder there and if you find it difficult to do any of these things, write to the Secretary of a specialist club – if you have a Siamese for example, the Secretary of the Siamese Cat Club or the Secretary of the Siamese Cat Association – who will be only too willing to help.

Once you have been in touch with a stud owner and have exchanged information as to the health, age and pedigree of your respective cats, you should then ask if you might visit the stud. This is most important. You must see the cat and the conditions under which he lives. All the points which I stressed in connection with hygiene when writing about buying your kitten apply again here.

Look at the cat himself, it will be obvious to you whether he is fit and active or sluggish and ill-kempt. See his quarters, and the place where your queen will be kept. This should be a clean spacious cage inside the male's house, containing a box, clean blanket, water bowl and fresh-looking litter tray. All being well, you must then make a tentative booking with the stud owner, arranging with her when she would like to be advised of your queen's next call.

When you have chosen your stud you must have your cat wormed immediately to ensure worm-free kittens, for she must be in first class condition. As soon as she shows the signs of calling, telephone the stud owner who will tell you when to bring her. Make absolutely sure your queen is well as it is the height of folly and deception to take a queen to a stud if she is off colour.

I always like owners to contact me as soon as they suspect their queen of coming into season, for it gives me an idea of exactly when to reserve the stud, whereas if I am not advised until two or three days after the start of the call, it can often be too late because I have accepted another queen.

It may well be that the stud you choose to use will live many miles away. It is still, in my opinion, of the greatest importance that you should visit the breeder before sending your cat to her. It is quite safe to send your queen by rail to the stud owner. So long as she is securely fastened in a strong box or basket, has no change en route, and is met by the stud owner at the other end, this is a good way to send your cat. I use the words 'securely fastened' because I once went to the station to meet a queen, only to be handed an empty basket! Both leather fastenings were still buckled, but so loosely that the queen had managed to squeeze herself through the space between the lid and the basket. I was most distressed when presented with the empty container, and the railway porters and the guard were equally concerned. The train had continued its journey and I arranged to wait until the train returned. As soon as it came into the station again, two porters and I searched that train from one end to the other, but with no result. The cat must have escaped either at my station or further down the line and was probably miles away in the country somewhere.

I immediately contacted the cat's owner, who agreed that she had not fastened the straps too tightly because she thought the cat would want to get her nose out for more air! The search continued until late at night as sidings and stations on the line were explored, with no results. Early next morning after a very restless night, I had a call from the railway station. A porter had found the cat at another station sitting in a luggage rack, happily watching the passengers alight. He realized she was temporarily ownerless and as he was just going off duty he lifted her down from the rack, tucked her into his coat and took her home and fed her. He knew nothing of the panic going on until next morning when returning for duty he brought her with him to see if she had been reported missing. I was so relieved when I heard that I forbore to criticize the porter for not informing the parcels office of his find. The eventful journey did not appear to affect the cat at all and she sub-sequently produced a beautiful litter of six kittens.

I believe some queens have love affairs like humans. A friend of mine has three queens, all of whom came regularly to my studs. One of them, called Samantha, had been a difficult little queen to mate as she was timid and unwilling. At that time I had a stud, Oakay, famous for his gentle temperament and affectionate nature. After unsuccessfully visiting several studs Samantha was brought to Oakay, and I truly believe it was love at first sight for they mated happily with no trouble at all.

Samantha had several beautiful litters from Oakay until one day he was not available when she quite suddenly decided to call. We tried her with first one and then another of my three studs, but each time she rejected them with much spitting and scratching. Eventually, although she was by this time well on in her call, Oakay was free and I took her into his house. Her joy on beholding him was almost pathetic. I put her down and she quickly snuggled up to him, looking with obvious adoration into his face, uttering loud 'Brrrs, Brrrs'. When eventually Oakay died, Samantha remained faithful to him and refused to have any more kittens.

Give your queen a good grooming before you take her to the stud; and if you are sending her by train be sure to make the fullest arrangements with the stud owner. Your queen will stay with her mate for two or three days and when you fetch her you will receive the stud's full pedigree, on which is usually written the date of mating and the approximate date of the kittens' birth. If your queen has not conceived at this mating, most stud owners are usually prepared to give you another free of charge.

The first time I brought a queen home after her visit to a stud I imagined she would settle down again into respectability and I remember feeling slightly disgusted with her when for two more days she continued to call. It had cost me a fair sized stud fee to buy her this visit to her husband and here she was announcing to all passers by that she was still 'available', although, as it turned out she was pregnant.

For three weeks there will be no outward sign of anything taking place. Some breeders say their queens have 'morning sickness', but the one thing I have noticed is that mine

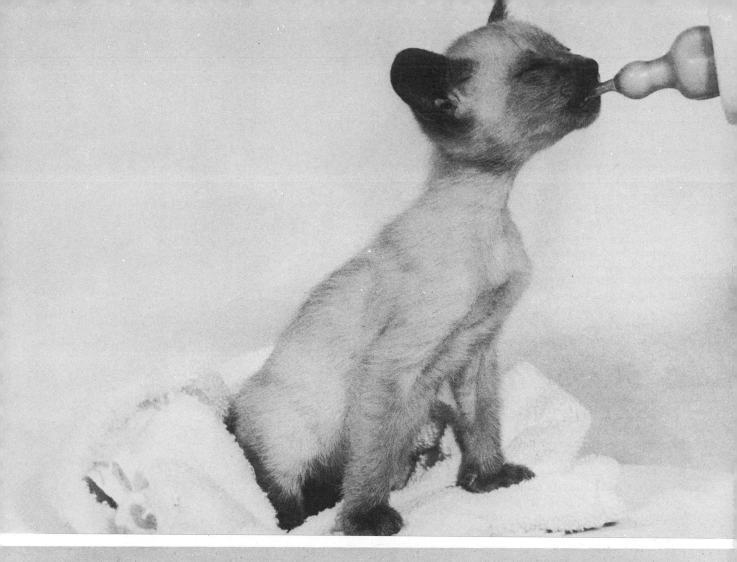

A Seal Point kitten about three weeks old which is being hand reared since the mother had more kittens than she could cope with.
Left, the kitten has just woken up and instantly thinks of food . . . and then below, sinks back into contented sleep after being fed.

sleep a lot for the first week or two. Whether this is Nature's way of compensating for the cat's loss of sleep whilst calling or whether, like some human mothers, they do require this sleep I do not know, but I am always very happy to witness their drowsiness and invariably it is a sign that my queen has 'taken'.

Try not to handle the cat more than you have to and do not allow others, particularly children, to do so, for at this stage the queen is vulnerable.

Experienced breeders can usually tell quite early on just by handling a cat whether she is in kitten, but you can usually know yourself three weeks after mating. However, as the time comes round when she would start her call if she had not been mated, watch carefully for a few days and if you are even remotely suspicious, keep her indoors where you can watch her. If she calls, it means you have to start the whole procedure over again, but it is not very likely that she will.

I have not so far mentioned diet during pregnancy, because for the first four weeks your queen will be having her three meals a day with no special additions, except for the daily vitamins. In the fourth week there are three alterations. You should add one teaspoonful daily of calcium lactate, or Cola Cal. D. The amount of protein should also be increased, so you must give extra meat, rabbit, fish, chicken or offal. If she will eat cheese in any form, give her a daily ration, for this will include calcium for the bones and teeth of the kittens as well as protein. Needless to say, do not overload her stomach with food, this is certainly not a help, but I suggest she now has four meals per day instead of three. Lastly I add some raspberry leaf tea. It has been used in childbirth by many races and it is said to make for an easier, quicker kittening. Its properties have been known for centuries and help to strengthen the uterus and stimulate the muscular contractions at birth thus ensuring a smooth delivery. I give half a teaspoon on food daily until the day of kittening.

As time passes, give her whatever amount of food she demands. A little and often is best for her; although she will be very hungry, there may not be much room left for her to digest it. Never give medicine to a pregnant cat unless directed by your vet. A little extra food and care is all that is needed for a healthy pregnancy and

the latter includes not allowing anyone, particularly children, to pick her up, and trying to prevent her from jumping from heights. I have a queen who spends most of her summer pregnancies on the roof! She is remarkably sure footed, but I am never very happy with her choice of resting place.

It is wise to tell your vet that you are expecting your cat to kitten on or around a certain date so that if you should need him, he has had notice of the event and will have made provision. A queen carries her kittens for 63 to 65 days, but it could be a day or two longer. She will want to spend

all her time with you or however much you can spare her. She will enjoy her pregnancy rolling in the sunshine, watching the birds, knocking your pencils off a table, and generally showing her joy in living, like all creatures who carry their young.

One grows very excited as the day for the kittening approaches, but your cat will show no apprehension; her instinct tells her something is going to happen, though she is not sure what.

You will see a picture of a box (Pg. 94) which I invented primarily for my queens to use when having their kittens. I found it so successful that I

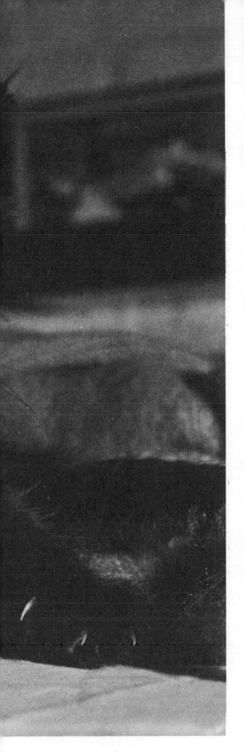

A stray which has been rescued and coddled, but is not quite happy yet.

used it for all my cats. It is easy to make, cheap to run, warm and fool-proof, and has been copied by many people including vets. The box is made of hardboard, measuring 14 by 14 inches. The base, fitted with re-movable peg board is painted under-neath with aluminium fire proof paint. The front lifts out, thus en-abling young kittens to get out of the box when ready. At one side an electric lead is inserted and a lamp holder fixed under the peg board floor which is then fitted with a light bulb. A piece of hardboard 14 by 20 inches is fitted into the box as illustrated, thus making a canopy which if

covered with a towel or blanket keeps the cat or kittens beautifully warm. I hope your queen will be as happy to use this box as are mine, even though there may have been a difference of opinion between you as to its suita-bility.

There always is a difference of opinion. Some cats even have their babies inside tree trunks! Others seem to think that eiderdowns, blankets and airing cupboards are the best places and can be very obstinate about it. Harden your heart. Eider-downs are quite unsuitable for kitten-ing, I know, it has happened to me. Try to convince your unco-operative

female that good renewable news-paper is more suitable as well as being cheaper than eiderdowns or blankets. Birth is an untidy business and news-paper is cheap, absorbent, and when it is all over, easily burnt.

It often happens that a cat is late in starting her labour and has shown no sign of doing so by the 65th day. There may be plenty of torn paper in her box, but she is eating well and if anything, is more skittish than ever. It is very worrying when the days pass and nothing happens, but it is best to wait if you can and allow her to go naturally into labour providing she appears well. If you do take her to the vet the first thing he will do is to take her temperature. If kittening is to be within the next few hours, the temperature will be falling. This is an infallible sign that the first stage of labour has begun, although she may have given no other indication. He will then examine her, feel how the kittens are lying, ask various questions, and probably tell you not to worry, all is well.

Some queens are very calm about it all and will quietly and without fuss find a cupboard in spite of your preparations, and will have their kittens before you are even aware of what is happening. Others, and perhaps the majority like to have people around, and make it quite clear they want you there for encouragement once they make the unmistakable signs of going into labour.

The queen will probably refuse food and if you have another cat in the house she will do her best to persuade her friend to settle in the kittening box with her, even to the extent of trying to grab the cat by the back of the neck. This is all quite normal, and if she succeeds in her attempt it will keep her reasonably happy for some time. If however she is an only cat, she will be restless, dashing frequently outside or to her litter tray, and crying plaintively whilst she vigorously tears paper for her nest.

Eventually, after several restless hours the queen will settle herself in her box or chosen bed as the second stage of labour begins. Contractions will gradually become stronger and it does seem the queen suffers little discomfort at this time, often purring noisily as you encourage her efforts. Sometimes at the moment of the first birth she gives a cry, but seldom with any following kittens.

Keep nearby a small rough towel, a hot water bottle, and a box of paper tissues. This is all you need. It may be that the first thing you see is not a head but a tail. Don't panic and forget all the horrors you read about breech births, and 'kittens the wrong way round'. In my experience many, many kittens are born this way, possibly 50 per cent, but providing you are there, encouraging your queen, equipped with the small rough towel with which to calmly assist, there is little to fear. It may require rather more contractions to expel a kitten the wrong way round, especially if it is the first, but in most cases she will manage on her own. If after two or three further contractions the kitten is not fully born and the head is still inside the queen take your small towel and with it grasp the little body gently and firmly from the shoulders enclosing as much of the head as your fingers can grip. When the next contraction comes, pull very gently towards the back of the queen and out will slip the kitten. This is important because if the kitten's head stays too long within the mother's body, it will suffocate.

Marjorie Hudson's Chocolate Point Siamese Queen nursing her family who are four days old.

Below, contented family.

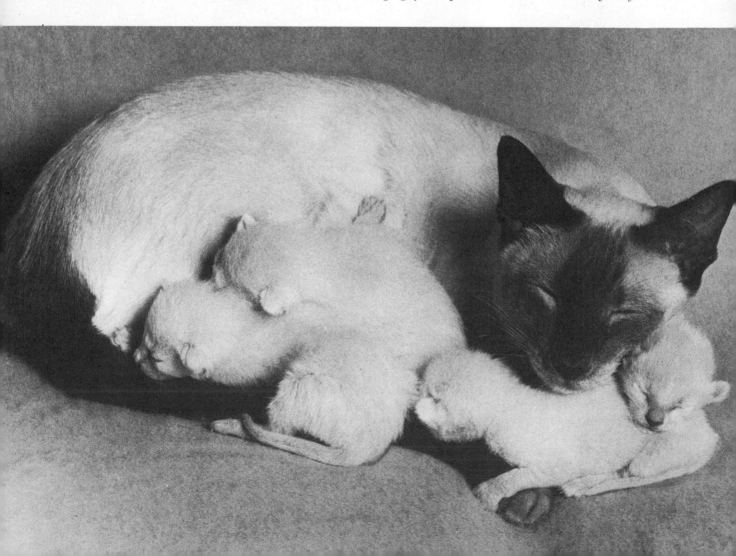

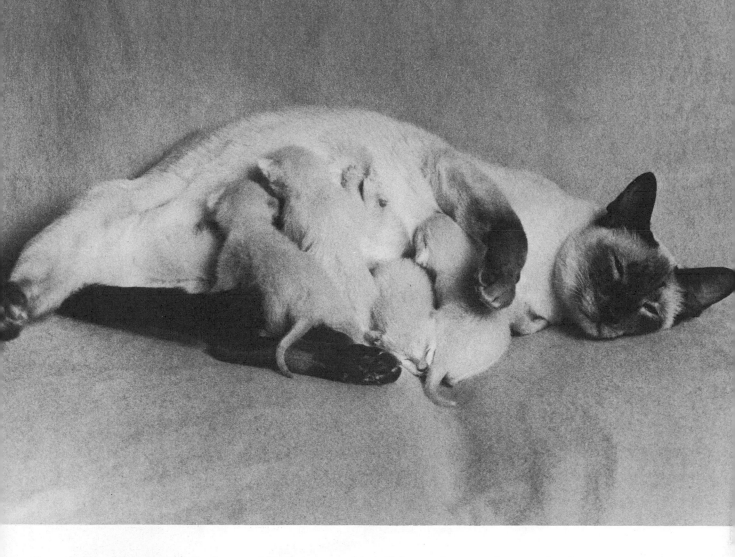

Immediately after the birth the queen will rupture the membranes herself and proceed vigorously to lick the kitten clean and dry. If, however, she appears hesitant, don't wait more than a few seconds before gently but quickly tearing a hole in the sac which completely encloses the kitten thus liberating it and allowing it to draw its first independent breath.

You will realize the kitten is still attached to the mother by the umbilical cord and the queen will almost certainly sever the cord herself, and then eat the placenta and afterbirth which contains valuable vitamins and hormones. Sometimes a nervous female, especially a maiden queen, will not sever the cord and this is then your first introduction to midwifery.

Don't be in any hurry to interfere, but if it is obvious the queen is not going to do it herself take the cord between the first finger and thumb of your right hand, holding the other end firmly in your left, about three inches from the kitten's body. Tear it gently but strongly across in a jagged cut using your scrubbed thumb nail. A rugged tear is better than a clean cut

with scissors, as this will lessen the amount of haemorrhage and drain away remaining fluid. Now offer your queen a warm drink, perhaps milk if she likes it, or Brand's Essence, or even plain water, as having babies is thirsty work.

The kittens should follow each other fairly rapidly, but there may be anything up to a two hour interval in between each arrival.

It is just possible that one kitten may arrive apparently lifeless. With your rough towel in your hand, pick up the little body, quietly so that you do not agitate the mother, and proceed to rub it vigorously with the towel across the back, head and legs, making sure the nose and mouth are free of any mucus, which might impede its breathing. If there is still no sign of life, this is the moment for drastic action. You will need courage and if I hadn't been taught by a wonderful vet, I would never have tried to follow his method. Run some hot water into a basin, as hot as you can bear to place your hand in, and in another basin some cold water. Grasp the kitten by the head, supporting it

with your other hand under the back legs and quickly 'dunk' it alternately into the hot and then the cold water. Do this four or five times and if there is a spark of life in its body the kitten will respond, suddenly uttering a cry and drawing up its back legs. This action may be repulsive to you, but if everything else fails it is a last hope.

The kittening over, you will have an exhausted 'mum' but a lovely litter.

By the next morning – although I am sure you have visited them during the night – the kittens will be fluffy, fat and feeding well. Mother, who has not left their side since the birth, will be fatuously happy, and herself beautifully clean, but you will probably need to change the paper in the box and in fact you can now put a blanket in if you wish.

Get a cardboard box, put a hot water bottle at the bottom, cover it with a blanket and then gently lift each kitten in. Do it calmly, talking reassuringly to your queen. When all are safely there, put the queen in too and proceed to clean up the bed. With a fresh blanket safely in place, you

can return first mother to her clean bed and then the kittens.

There is nothing more for you to do except keep a watchful eye on mother and babies, making sure the former is eating and drinking well and that the babies are suckling. The surest way of telling whether all is well is the sight of a bundle of tiny bodies and absolutely no sound. If there is a sickly baby among the litter, the queen will know instinctively and

deal with the little thing in her own fashion – she will either lie on it or push it out into the cold, and you will be wiser not to interfere with that instinct.

Warmth is the most important aspect of a kitten's survival, and chills are responsible for a large proportion of early deaths. Kittens, after all, have been kept at an even temperature within the mother's body and that temperature needs to be

Here she is carrying one by the scruff of its neck. Notice that her coat is unshaded on the back, which is quite an achievement for a cat who leads a normal life outside and in the house.

maintained. Do not overheat mother or kittens, but constant gentle heat is essential, hence my partiality for my heated box where the warmth is gentle and can be regulated by the size of the electric bulb.

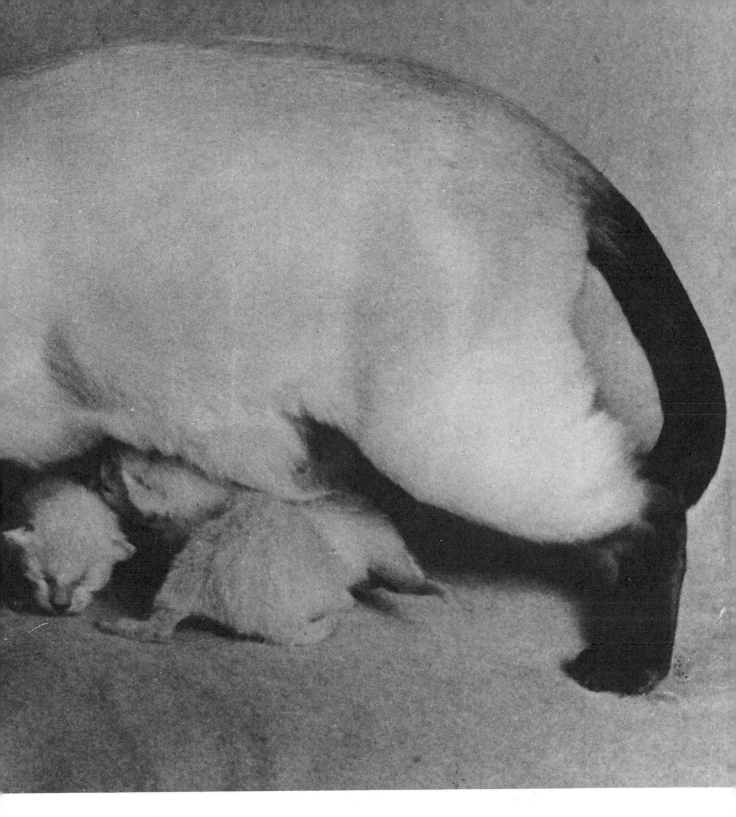

All the foregoing is the average kittening of most queens. There are other difficulties and complications but as I have already said, this book was not intended as a veterinary reference and if you have doubts about anything connected with your kittens or cat, do not hesitate to contact your vet. Keep your queen quiet and isolated – and let her get on with the business of rearing her family.

When they are seven to ten days old their eyes will begin to open and although they cannot focus it is an exciting event and they begin to develop quickly from this moment. Around three weeks of age you will notice the kittens moving freely around their box. It is then that the joys and responsibilities of breeding begin in earnest.

If the queen has a large litter – six or seven kittens – they will readily accept your efforts to gradually wean them. If there are only three or four, then they will be less interested, for the mother will have plenty with which to feed her babies. Try at three or three and a half weeks to introduce a milk mixture. One I always use and which I find the kittens and their mother soon enjoy is unsweetened evaporated milk, boiled water and glucose: two parts milk, one part water, with half a teaspoonful of glucose.

Place a little on a flat plate, put the first kitten at the side, dip your clean finger into the milk and place it on the kitten's mouth and nose. In a short time he will get the taste and when that happens gradually lower your finger on to the plate and invariably the kitten continues to lap. Treat each in turn until in a day or two the kittens are happily lapping on their own. I do not use a spoon, because I find tiny kittens dislike the cold hard texture of metal and will more readily take from a finger. I never push a kitten's nose into the food as this so often causes it to splutter and take fright and that means a delay in weaning. Never force the process of weaning. It will come if you have patience, but it will come when the kitten decides and only then. A burst of irritability on your

part will put the kitten back for days, so if you cannot spare the time or have not the patience, leave it a day or two and then try again.

After three or four days have passed with the kittens freely lapping, add a little Farlene to the milk and so thicken it to a creamy texture. The kittens will love it. At this stage add one drop of Adexolin, increasing every second day by one drop until for each kitten, one drop daily is added, so that for a litter of four for example you will eventually be adding four drops daily. All utensils and plates must be well washed and boiled after each meal. Never leave food on a plate for the next meal. Bacteria grows rapidly in milk substances and these in turn lead to gastric infections.

At around five weeks add a little steamed fish to the milk, using the fish

The same family at four and a half weeks old. It can now be seen that there are two Chocolate Point and two Seal Point kittens – the Seal Points have darker shading on their backs while the other two have none.

water to make up the food, and a few days later, half the yolk of an egg. At six weeks, finely minced, lean, raw beef may be introduced and if at first the kittens turn up their noses at the smell or texture, try mixing it with a little of their evaporated milk. Gradually decrease the milk and increase the meat, and once they get used to this you are well away. All this demands time and patience, but there are few interests in life quite so rewarding as watching the growth

Previous page and left, the family at seven and a half weeks old . . . and they are unlikely to give their Mother much peace.

The Chocolate Point kitten in the front (top left) and far right (below) is an exceptionally beautiful kitten with large, widely spaced ears and long face.

Above and right, two Red Point kittens aged six months with their mother. These cats have points of a lovely red gold colour, though this will not yet be fully developed on their legs.

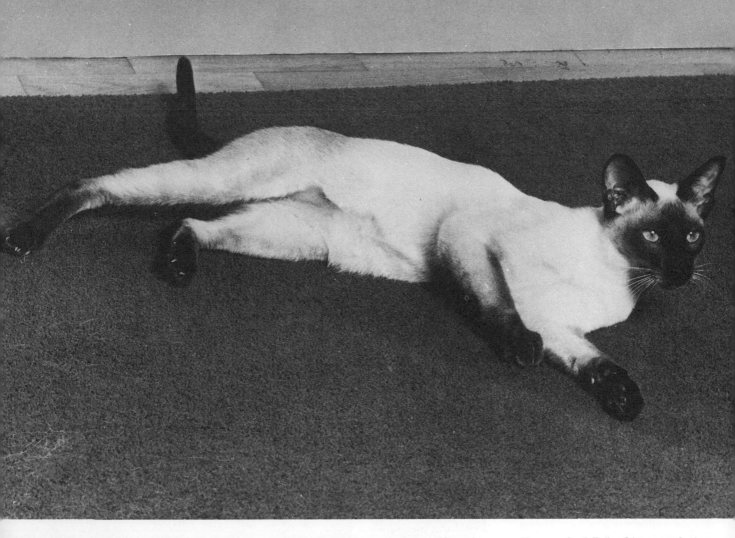

of tiny creatures and kittens are no exception.

Two warnings. It is a known fact among breeders that marauding Toms will, if they can reach them, kill any or all the kittens in a litter. I have known this tragedy happen to two different litters, so keep your kittens where they cannot be found by strange, often half wild, male cats. Children also have to be watched as they can be over-enthusiastic and kittens need a lot of sleep. Of course, they will love the kittens and will naturally want to see and touch and eventually hold the kittens but not for too long and not too violently. Children will be fascinated by the devotion and discipline maintained by your queen and I know of no finer teacher than a mother cat. Children have to learn the responsibilities of keeping a pet but it is up to you to supervise those lessons and especially whilst a young inexperienced mother is nursing her first litter. As the kittens grow daily more enchanting, children long to participate in their play, and

this is fine as long as they realize the dangers of dropping or frightening them.

Sexing the kittens is best done by a knowledgeable breeder or your veterinary surgeon. At seven weeks the queen should begin to leave her kittens for longer periods and it is a good idea to start this by removing her at night. By the time they are ready for inoculation at ten weeks old she will have grown used to the idea of their departure, unless you intend to keep one of them as her permanent companion.

Inoculation

At nine weeks, arrange with your veterinary surgeon for your litter to be inoculated against F I E . If he can and will come to your home for this purpose, well and good. I never like taking un-inoculated kittens to a vet's surgery and if I have to I leave them in the basket outside the surgery until the vet is ready for them. I feel some risks are avoided by these methods. Whichever way it is to be,

Above, a Seal Point kitten aged nine months. Although almost fully grown, he has yet to fill out into a cat.

Right, a perfect match in colouring if not in size . . .

your kittens must be inoculated at ten weeks – not sooner, and definitely not later, for by this time the immunity conferred to the babies by the mother has disappeared, and once that has happened every kitten is at risk from this kitten disease.

I believe that every person who allows kittens to be brought into the world – pedigree or otherwise – has a responsibility towards those kittens. Not only should each kitten have a good foundation with the right food and adequate love and attention, but they should go to reliable homes as

far as this can be ensured. If I sell a
kitten I insist on meeting the prospective buyer and not only discussing
the matter with her, but watching her
reaction to the kittens. I have a
number of stipulations from which I
absolutely cannot be moved.

I will never sell an only kitten to a
person or people who are out working
all day. I was once asked for a kitten
by someone who already had several
cats, but whom I knew left her home
at 7.30 am until 7.00 pm. I asked how
she proposed to feed it and her reply
was that in her family night turns
into day. The cats get a meal at 8.00
pm, another at 1.00 am, and the last
at 7.00 am, and that they all thrive.

Perhaps they do, but I prefer rather
more orthodox methods of feeding,
so my kittens didn't go there. I will
sell two kittens to anyone if they can
arrange feeding midday, but again,
never one solitary kitten. I think the
sudden change of environment and
owners and the separation from its
family is shock enough for a kitten
without the addition of complete
solitude all day.

I always like to see the reaction of
children with a kitten. It can be a
nine days wonder or it can be love at
first sight. By now I have developed
a sixth sense and if for any reason
this instinct of mine goes to work
against selling the kitten to a particu-

lar person, then somehow, without hurting feelings, I have to refuse. I once asked a young couple who wanted a kitten to call and see me and the litter. They arrived in complete motor cycle gear. I questioned them on their intentions because I was slightly uneasy. Everything seemed all right; yes, the wife was at home all day; yes, she had read all about Siamese and had longed for one ever since she had been married. I racked my brain for an excuse to delay a decision about the kitten but the more off-putting I was, the keener she became. However, I managed to suggest she should go away, talk it over with her husband and 'phone me if she decided she was still keen. Just as they were leaving, she turned to me and said, 'Oh, by the way – we go motor cycling every Sunday, I hope a Siamese will *stay* in a saddle bag?' Needless to say – mine would not!

Above, a tale of woe or a huge joke? Whichever it is this kitten is definitely quite a character.

Right, an early attempt to get at the top of the milk.

Boarding catteries

I am presuming you have raised your kitten towards adulthood. Suddenly you are faced with a problem. You are going to fix the family holiday and what is to happen to your precious kitten? You cannot take him with you for a number of reasons. First, if you are going abroad you would be unable to bring him back into this country without a period of six months in quarantine and that is out of the question. Secondly, if you are spending your holiday in England, there are few hotels which will encourage you to bring your cat, and even if you were allowed to take him it is unlikely that he would like being in a strange room unable to have his freedom and forced to eat food to which he is not accustomed. So he has to stay behind.

Having come to this conclusion you may think your neighbours will have him, but this is not reliable as they too may be going away. Perhaps a friend will be able to come in and feed him every day, and this is the solution that many people come to. However, it is not much fun for the kitten. You go off on an enjoyable holiday while he is shut up all alone without any company. This is where having two kittens is a very good idea because when you do go away they will not be lonely, but on the whole it is never very satisfactory to have to rely on a friend who will probably be busy.

The best solution is a Boarding Cattery if you can find a good one. There are dozens of them of all sizes, shapes and conditions. It is not difficult to find a place to board your pet, but for every good one, there are twenty bad! Look in your local paper, ask your vet and between them you should get some addresses even if no real information. Most vets know the good and bad catteries, and many of them have lists in their waiting rooms, but don't expect them to have inspected every cattery. There is one necessary and infallible way of find-

A kitten born on a farm is often independent and adventurous by the time he is four or five months old.

ing out what conditions are like: go to the cattery you may consider using. Remember that your cat will be there for quite a time and how can you enjoy your holiday unless you are happy about him?

Perhaps this is the moment to tell you how I came to start my boarding cattery. I certainly had no intention of doing so, but one day I was visiting a vet with a friend and whilst waiting I heard the unmistakable voice of a Siamese. I got up and wandered in the direction of the sound, saw an attendant and asked her if she had a sick Siamese there. 'Oh, no', she replied, 'come and have a look – it is one of the cats left here while his owners are away.' I went into a room lined with cages. In one of them there sat the most miserable Siamese male. There was barely room for more than himself and a sanitary tray, and in that cage this cat was to spend two cramped unhappy weeks. I returned home, determined to find some way of improving the lot of a few cats anyway and as we were fortunate to have a large amount of ground, it was comparatively easy.

Let me now tell you what to look for in a good boarding cattery. Every cat should be in a separate house of his own (unless you have two cats who live together) with sufficient space for him to wander. The house itself

This kitten has just pounced on a leaf in the grass and is reproaching the photographer for his failure to find a mouse.

should be warm, weather proof and light, with some form of heating should the weather turn cold or wet. Remember, your cat will be confined, so he must be warm because he isn't getting much exercise. He must be kept interested; a bored cat can get into unexpected mischief. He must be well fed for he will look forward to his meals far more than at home, where he has other means of passing his time. Ideally, there should be a window in the house, with a shelf beneath, to enable him to watch the outside world should it be wet.

In his garden there should be a scratching post, so that he may keep his claws in trim, with another shelf for sunbathing, allowing him to remain off the ground in damp weather. Every boarding cattery should have escape runs attached to the cat houses. In other words, the door of the cat house must be entered through an outer door which can be closed by the attendant before the cat's door is opened.

Look well at the litter trays provided. Ask if your cat's diet can and will be followed and whether a vet is within call. At the same time, ask what their record is for illness or whether they have ever had a cat escape and why. An almost infallible rule is the appearance of the owner or attendant. If those in charge are clean, alert and kindly and their own living conditions good, their cattery will almost certainly be satisfactory.

Take your cat to the cattery in his basket, never in your arms. He may take fright from the noise of other cats or the unfamiliar catty smells. If possible take with you any toy or toys which are his special property, and whatever you do, don't give him a tranquillizer for these are often very unsatisfactory for cats or kittens. Many owners ask their vet to give their cat a sedative when about to travel. These will often have quite

garden at all hours. The sheer glee on their faces was most amusing but as I was responsible for these two rascals I eventually wired the fastening at night, preventing them from opening it.

Late one night I was doing my 'rounds' in a downpour before going to bed, and was just congratulating myself that at least I could be sure that 'those two' would be unable to get out and catch cold, when my torch picked up what looked like four little green headlights. I couldn't believe my eyes, but it was Cleo and Clary out again. Determined not to be beaten they had walked through the glass of their window, pieces of which still remained on their soaking coats. I'll swear those cats were grinning when I picked them up! It took me an hour to nail hardboard against their window and another ten minutes to call a message into their owner's 'Ansafone', requesting their removal next day and disclaiming any further responsibility!

Don't be afraid to call on a boarding cattery without an appointment. This is expected by good owners who have nothing to hide and will gladly show you around. Don't be afraid to ask questions and tell the owner all you can about your cat. Places to be avoided are those which have cages and particularly places where there are several cages under one roof. When there are several cats under a single roof, although without actual contact, only one has to sneeze and all those around are infected. Every year catteries have to close because of cat 'flu and usually it arises because of overcrowding or lack of hygiene. Cats should never have to share a building with other unknown cats, for whereas older cats may have a natural immunity to most diseases, younger animals do not have this advantage and will succumb more quickly to any bug going around.

All houses must be empty for a minimum of 24 hours between occupants. This gives time for complete scrubbing and fumigation – very necessary if one is to be sure of disease-free accommodation for an incoming visitor. I would never send a cat where dogs also were boarding. Many cats are terrified of dogs and the noise they make. A cat needs specialized treatment from cat lovers and must, therefore, be exclusively catered for.

The old adage 'You get what you pay for' is in this situation very true.

the opposite effect on the cat, who becomes excited and hysterical. If a fairly heavy dose is given the cat often becomes extremely 'dopey' and difficult to arouse, and there is a danger of pneumonia becoming a serious side effect. Aspirin is lethal to cats and should never be given under any circumstances.

Cats are known to be escapologists, but even so I didn't bargain for the pranks of two who came to us whilst their owners went away. Cleo and Clary lived together in one house, sharing a basket under an infra red lamp. As it was mid-summer, they didn't need their heating – at least I

didn't think it was necessary, as it was during an August heatwave. Cleo and Clary, however, thought otherwise and every morning one or the other had managed to switch on the lamp. There they would be stretched full length, soporific with warmth, their eyes fixed upon me to see my reaction to their cleverness. After several days of this I had to remove the bulb altogether.

Baulked of this game they found another, and worked out a method of opening their window. They worked on the horizontal fastening until they managed to lift it and open the window, thus having free access to their

An Abyssinian Kitten.

No one can care for, feed and efficiently run a cattery for nothing. Therefore spend as much as you can on your kitten's/cat's holiday accommodation. Most really good places demand a certificate saying when your kitten was inoculated against Feline Infectious Enteritis. If it was more than a year before, you will probably be asked to take him for a 'Booster'. Do this willingly; it is well worth it.

If and when you have decided where to lodge your cat for his holiday, do book early. The best places, like the best hotels, quickly become full and unless you are able to make an early booking, it may mean you will be disappointed and will have to take second best. Do keep the cattery rules. Running a boarding establishment is a most demanding job which often entails working 14 hours a day for 365 days a year. If the cattery hours are from 8.00 am to 8.00 pm don't try collecting your cat at 9.00 pm or, as has so often happened to me, knock up the poor proprietor at midnight, because you happen to be on your way home. Always book an adequate length of time, for in the holiday season (and sometimes all the year round in many catteries) bookings are so closely worked out that if a cat is uncollected for 24 hours over the stated period, the distracted organizer is faced with chaos! I had a regular client who brought his cat each year, delivering and collecting her as arranged. One year he didn't arrive to collect and at the end of a worrying fortnight I telephoned his home. He answered the 'phone himself, and on my asking why he hadn't collected the cat, he explained quite casually that he had been busy and

didn't think it mattered! Needless to say, we never again accepted his cat.

If you make a booking at a cattery, confirm the dates in writing, sending a deposit. If for any reason you find yourself unable to keep to the date of admittance, do 'phone the cattery owner; don't just not turn up. If you have a spiteful or difficult cat, tell the cattery owner. She would sooner know, for then she is prepared to deal with such a cat. Most of these cases are due to a cat being intensely nervous and it is a strange animal who cannot be won over. We were once asked to board a brown Bur-

mese for a very charming young couple. In absolute honesty they told us 'Ching' had only once before been to a cattery. Half way through their holiday they were summoned back by the cattery owner who told them she was petrified of the cat and could do nothing with her.

I was not very keen to take Ching, but promised to try her for three weeks. It was the longest three weeks I have ever known. Ching would wait until her door was opened in the morning and then as quick as lightning, she would grab a leg or a foot, or even a hand or arm with both claws

Above, 'Please I want to come in'. Right, Chinchilla kitten at a show. They are understandably one of the most popular cats of all as their coats have a silvery sparkle and their eyes are emerald green with black rims.

and teeth. The only way we could change her box was to put in her dish of food with one hand, sliding out the sanitary tray and replacing it with a clean one whilst she was eating.

On the morning when her owners were due to collect her, Ching paced up and down her run like a little brown

Left, playing under the table . . . and above, a Seal Point sound asleep.

lioness. She wouldn't eat, she didn't even spit and nothing could stop the restless pacing. At four o'clock a car drew up and Ching's owners arrived. That little cat was like one possessed. I quickly told the young couple we simply couldn't have her again and that they must themselves remove her from her house. The man went into Ching's cat garden. She immediately jumped upon his shoulder, nibbled

his ear and, completely unrestrained, came towards me. Imagine my horror when without hesitation and leadless she was abruptly transferred to my shoulder. I stood still, thinking she would tear my face or claw my eyes; but not a bit of it, she bent down, kissed my nose and purring fit to burst, tenderly nibbled my ear.

Of course we had her again, several times each year in fact, and the performance was repeated each time. She always knew the day of her owner's return and no matter how awful she was whilst in captivity, once she was collected she would revert to her real sweet self, begging my under-

standing with kisses and many other winning ways.

I once had two cats coming to stay for two months, after which they were to go by air to Singapore. The whole arrangement was made over the telephone, which is never very satisfactory, and the cats duly arrived from London by train. I collected them, took them home and on lifting them out for examination, found a long-haired Ginger female and a Seal Point Siamese unneutered male! I was horrified, because I had not been told that one of the cats was an 'entire' male. I should have asked, of course, but such a possibility had not occur-

red to me once during our talks.

I telephoned the owner, who was quite casual about it, until I asked if she realized they might mate together. Such a thought had not entered her head but she assured me that they had been together for more than two years and nothing had happened and that they dearly loved each other. I was not allowed to separate or neuter either of the cats, so I kept my fingers crossed and hoped.

One morning, six weeks later, I went to open their house and found not two loving cats, but six! There had been four kittens born to the pair during that night and both mum and dad were in the same box caring for the multi-coloured kits, who were spotless and dry. I am certain no human father was ever more delighted with his firstborn than that sweet and gentle Tom. Needless to say, it was weeks before they could travel, but as soon as the kittens were old enough, all six went off to their

delighted owner in Singapore.

I have also had cats with the oddest fads and fancies in food. One likes strawberries and cucumber and seems to know when they are in season. Another owner demands melon for her cat; we try to oblige, but it makes life somewhat complicated for the poor cattery owner. Owners often worry about their cat's reaction to a cattery. I can assure you all, I have never had a cat pine to the extent of refusing food for more than 24 hours. Many owners, I am sure, are greatly disappointed to find their cats have not only survived but have actually been happy enough not to pine.

Cats come into boarding catteries for many reasons. Sometimes during their 'call', to keep them safe from mismating; sometimes for correction of diet. If your cat suddenly develops a taste for smoked salmon and steadfastly refuses all else, what do you do? Send him to your favourite cattery where understanding people gently

Above, two black and white cats posing. Right, a Long-haired Silver Tabby and her playful kitten.

but firmly wean him from his expensive taste.

I hope I have convinced you that a good cattery is the best solution to the problem of leaving your kittens and cats. Furthermore, if you are convinced, it should follow that the major drawback to having a kitten – the fact that the owner is tied – has been eliminated and so there is nothing to put you off and everything to recommend your having a pet or pets. It remains for you to make your choice and then reap all the enjoyment that I am sure you will from owning one of these most attractive and delightful animals.

Acknowledgement

Blue Cross Animals Hospital, London   95.
Bruce Coleman Ltd.   77, 81.
Colour Library International   21, 70–1, 82, 119.
Anne Cumbers   39, 79.
Radio Times Hulton Picture Library   68, 86–7.
Pictorial Press   6–8, 14–19, 26–30, 35, 36, 38, 43, 4.
    50–7, 65–7, 74–6, 88–9, 91, 96–8, 122–5, 129, 135.
Picture Point Ltd.   10–11, 22 top.
Spectrum Colour Library   9, 12 top, 20, 22 bottom,
    24, 25, 42, 48, 49, 59, 64, 69, 92, 93, 101, 102, 132.
Syndication International   66–7, 73, 120.
Sally Anne Thompson   13, 23, 31–4, 37, 39–41, 44,
    46, 47, 60–3, 72, 78, 80, 83–5, 90, 94, 95, 99, 100,
    104–115, 121, 126–8, 130, 131, 133.
Barbara Woodhouse   12.